# OTHER BOOKS BY THOMAS L. QUICK

Your Role in Task Force Management:
*The Dynamics of Corporate Change (1972)*

The Ambitious Woman's Guide to a Successful Career
*(with Margaret V. Higginson, 1975)*

Understanding People at Work (1976)

Person to Person Managing (1977)

The Quick Motivation Method (1980)

The Persuasive Manager:
*How to Sell Yourself and Your Ideas (1982)*

Boosting Employee Performance Through Better Motivation (1983)

Executive Assertiveness (1983)

Increasing Your Sales Success:
*1001 Ways to Excel in Selling (1984)*

Managing People at Work Desk Guide (1984)

The Manager's Motivation Desk Book (1985)

Power Plays (1985)

Inspiring People at Work:
*How to Make Participative Management Work for You (1986)*

Quick Solutions:
*500 People Problems Managers Face & How to Solve Them (1987)*

How People Work Best (1988)

Power, Influence, and Your Effectiveness in Human Resources (1988)

Managing for Peak Performance (1989)

Unconventional Wisdom:
*Irreverent Solutions for Tough Problems at Work (1989)*

Getting Good Results from Problem Employees:
*How to Turn Around Poor Job Performance (1990)*

Mastering the Power of Persuasion:
*How to Get the Results You Want on the Job (1990)*

# Training Managers
*So They Can*
# Really Manage

■ *Thomas L. Quick* ■

# Training Managers
## *So They Can*
# Really Manage

■                                                    ■

*Confessions*
*of a*
*Frustrated Trainer*

 Jossey-Bass Publishers
San Francisco   •   Oxford   •   1991

TRAINING MANAGERS SO THEY CAN REALLY MANAGE
*Confessions of a Frustrated Trainer*
    by Thomas L. Quick

Copyright © 1991 by:  Jossey-Bass Inc., Publishers
                      350 Sansome Street
                      San Francisco, California 94104

                            &

                      Jossey-Bass Limited
                      Headington Hill Hall
                      Oxford OX3 0BW

**Library of Congress Cataloging-in-Publication Data**

Quick, Thomas L.
    Training managers so they can really manage : confessions of a
frustrated trainer / Thomas L. Quick.
        p.    cm.—(The Jossey-Bass management series)
    Includes bibliographical references and index.
    ISBN 1-55542-341-8
    1. Executives—Training of—United States.   I. Title.
II. Series.
HD38.25.U6Q53      1991
658.4'07124—dc20                                        90-28765
                                                          CIP

Manufactured in the United States of America

The paper in this book meets the guidelines for
permanence and durability of the Committee on
Production Guidelines for Book Longevity of the
Council on Library Resources.

JACKET DESIGN BY MICHAEL MARTIN

FIRST EDITION
*HB Printing*         10 9 8 7 6 5 4 3 2
*Code 9144*

# ■ Contents ■

# ■ Preface ■

This book has a simple, ironic theme: we waste enormous amounts of money each year in the United States in the training and development of supervisors and managers. The objective of management training and development is to help managers manage people effectively. The evidence seems overwhelming that we fail to reach that objective much, if not most, of the time. Obviously, pouring record amounts of money into management training and development does not guarantee good results. Neither, apparently, does all of the magnificent research into the behavior of people at work that has been done during the thirty years I've been in the field. The money is there. The knowledge is there. We have the means to produce the best managers in the world. But I can't believe that anyone in management or in training can say with a straight face that we are producing them.

This appalling failure is no secret. Anyone who has worked with American managers over the past thirty years, as I have, must be aware that most managers, even those from well-known businesses, have a rather primitive understanding of what an effective manager is and how he or she practices managerial skills. Many of my professional training colleagues, people I admire and give much credence to, will (quietly, over a drink) acknowledge that traditional management training approaches have proved very disappointing.

No, it isn't a secret, but it's not surprising that people don't want to talk about it publicly.

Meanwhile, American businesses are facing fierce competition from their compatriots as well as from abroad. The time has passed when an executive could say, as I heard frequently in the 1970s, "We're going to make money whatever we do." I think it is no exaggeration to say that many of our businesses are moving from protecting their profit margins to trying to ensure their survival in these new and tough economic times.

It is time to speak candidly and without reservation about our shortcomings in producing good managers in this country and about what can be done to counteract them. Just as there is no secret about the past, there is no mystery about what can be done in the future to develop effective managers. I have written this book in full confidence that we can do the job that so far we have not done.

## Audiences

*Training Managers So They Can Really Manage* was written for several audiences. I hope each of them reads and heeds the messages. First, the book is aimed at corporate managers who authorize and evaluate training for supervisors and managers at all levels. For these people, the book provides a cost-effective approach to training that will also increase its impact. I offer a method to help these managers work constructively with training departments in designing and delivering training that will improve the effectiveness of their managers and supervisors. Second, the book is aimed at human resource development (HRD) and personnel professionals who are responsible for creating and implementing management development training programs. They will find in this book a relatively simple method for developing strong learning partnerships with managers that will increase the managers' credibility and effectiveness. In addition, the book provides specific help in designing relevant training programs and increasing the power and influence of these programs in the organization. Finally, I hope that some university teachers of training, human resource development, and other important management development courses will use this book to challenge their students to think about these issues before the fledgling professionals become immersed in the "real life" of corporate environments.

Previously, this book would have been directed to HRD professionals as the primary audience, but that, I think, has been part of the problem. The managers who pay for and authorize training for their managerial subordinates are the people who most need guidance in making that training pay off. So I have departed from tradition and written this book primarily for my managerial colleagues and secondarily for my training colleagues.

### Overview of the Contents

*Training Managers So They Can Really Manage* contains prescriptions for successful management training and development. The book consists of three parts. First, we look at the current training scene. My colleagues and I identify several traditional management training practices and explain why they have produced such disappointing results. In the second part, I draw on my thirty years of experience as a manager and management trainer to offer a six-step program for trainers and managers who authorize training. The steps aren't difficult in themselves—they just aren't the norm. But they make a lot of sense, knowing what we do about how adults learn and what motivates people to perform at their best. In my six steps, developed over the past several years in answer to my own frustrations, I strongly emphasize partnerships and collaboration among trainers, clients, and trainees.

Some of the steps are at present rarely taken—for example, the use of learning contracts between managers and their subordinates who are to be trained. What will happen as a result of the training? The goal should be clear before training begins. As a part of the contract, the manager takes responsibility for making sure that the trainee has a chance to practice what the trainer has preached. This is the point at which much training fails. Without application of the training content, there is probably no real learning; and with the accompanying memory loss, everything in the department soon returns to status quo ante. The completion of the learning contract should be the reward for successful application and practice. Whether you are a manager or a trainer, you may not realize what a potent force for change you have in rewards that are given wisely and justly.

Trainers may be surprised to learn that management training should take place in the context of motivation and that motivation (often presented as a subset of a training module on, say, leadership) is the book, not the chapter. Training managers in employee motivation confers instant relevance and practical value.

In the third part, we move on to the tools needed to implement an effective training program. If you are tempted to wonder whether the six steps are nice in theory, but . . . , read how one well-known firm, Johnson & Higgins, the giant insurance brokerage, is putting the six steps into practice. In addition, vice-president Karen Stein-Townsend provides an excellent road map for anyone who wants to know how to run a training operation that has impact. In this section, I advocate, as I have for years, the training of all managers in basic selling skills, even though they do not see themselves as salespeople. I also recommend that we resurrect assertiveness training to help managers communicate more effectively and negotiate more profitably. Finally, I direct your eyes to the very near future, to the new economic and working world that is taking form all around us, a world for which we must adjust our training perspectives.

## Background

The management training field has changed substantially since I entered it in the late fall of 1961, when I became a salesman for the Research Institute of America (RIA). At that time, the institute was publishing executive, supervisory, and sales self-development programs. Shortly afterward, it added a management membership for middle and upper-level managers. In those days, typical supervisory and management development material was fairly basic. The RIA material, usually in the form of newsletters, did not reflect the psychological research that had recently been undertaken in the workplace, but that would soon change as a result of some significant publishing. In fact, in the 1960s there was a quantum leap in the extent of our knowledge about people at work.

For those of us entering the work force in the 1950s, the

prevailing values were those described in William H. Whyte's (1956) book *The Organization Man*. The corporate structure was a pyramid, with the authority centralized at the top. Managers generally regarded their employees as rather simple in makeup. They married, bought houses and cars, took vacations. There was ample job security, as long as employees adopted the values of the corporation. Those values, which we now refer to as "the culture," generally defined how you dressed, related to others, and behaved in the workplace.

Chris Argyris, at that time a professor at Yale, studied organizational life in the 1950s. In his *Executive Leadership* (1953), he describes what it was like being a supervisor in those days. The supervisors in the company that Argyris studied, who were fairly typical in my experience, were very dependent on their bosses. Communication was largely vertical, not horizontal. Supervisors had little reward or punishment power—this was retained by those at higher levels. At their level, the supervisors technically were part of management, but in reality they had little connection with people higher up in the hierarchy and did not identify with them. They were acquiescent, subordinating their personal goals and values to those of the organization. Argyris used the word *intellective* to describe the atmosphere: Rationality was rewarded; expressions of emotion were frowned upon.

Motivating forces in people were seen as rather uncomplicated. You worked to make money, to get ahead, to build job security. However, that view of employee motivation was about to be challenged. In 1954, Abraham Maslow, a professor of psychology at Brandeis, published *Motivation and Personality*, in which he set forth the famous hierarchy of needs. We start at the bottom level with physiological needs—eating, drinking, sleeping, sex—and as these are satisfied we move up the hierarchy to fill other needs—safety, belongingness and love, esteem, and finally self-actualization.

Most people working in corporations didn't know about Maslow. At least there was no critical mass. But that changed in the early 1960s. Douglas McGregor, a professor at M.I.T., published his classic *The Human Side of Enterprise* in 1960, and soon we were all talking about Theory X and Theory Y. Managers who held

Theory X views of employees believed that most people really didn't want to work, that they had to be coerced, threatened with punishment, and closely directed. But those who held Theory Y assumptions knew that people found meaning in their work, that for the most part they sought responsibility instead of ducking it, and that they would willingly commit themselves to the achievement of organizational goals.

Another name appeared, that of Frederick Herzberg, a social scientist who had done work in motivation. He invented the two-factor theory, which explains that people are motivated by achievement, recognition of achievement, the work itself, responsibility, and possibility for growth and advancement. People are not motivated by salary or good supervision or job security or good working conditions, he said, although if they don't have these, they are dissatisfied.

In the 1960s, almost everyone who talked or wrote about management had to invoke the names of Maslow, Herzberg, and McGregor. I rather irreverently dubbed them the holy trinity. What was significant for those of us in the management development field was that managing people had quickly become much more complex than we had thought. For those of us who were writing about management (in 1966 I had joined the professional staff of RIA and now wrote instead of sold), those were heady times. There was always something new to write about. We were discovering what management was really about.

Rensis Likert, director of the Institute for Social Research at the University of Michigan, published *New Patterns of Management* in 1961, in which he offered evidence that most people worked more effectively in organizations in which a participative style of managing prevailed. In 1964, Robert R. Blake and Jane S. Mouton introduced us to the details of *The Managerial Grid*. Managers flocked to their Grid seminars, where they discovered how great was their concern for production over people and vice versa. The Grid provided a different kind of training, more experiential. Suddenly the *group* was the in thing. We had sensitivity training, encounter groups, marathon groups, and what was called the instrumented lab, where you worked in groups, observed group dynamics, learned how to give feedback to one another by using written instruments, and did some team building.

One book published in 1964 was to influence the rest of my life: *Work and Motivation,* by Victor H. Vroom, a professor at Yale. Vroom defined the Expectancy Theory of motivation, which eventually formed the basis for all of my work in training managers to manage the motivation of their employees. At about that time, Peter Drucker, a brilliant teacher and consultant, talked about effectiveness rather than efficiency, and managing by results or objectives. A professor at the University of Michigan, George Odiorne, picked up on the managing by objectives (MBO) concept, published a book, *Management by Objectives* (1965), and became a guru in the field.

Meanwhile, as a young man learning to write about management and to manage as well at RIA, I dashed around the country to various seminars, courses, and workshops on managing. I joined the American Society for Training and Development (ASTD) (which had recently changed its name from the American Society of Training Directors) and the almost brand-new National Organization Development Network, whatever that was. (About all I knew at first was that a number of people I respected greatly were joining.) In time I would come to understand that organization development (OD) would involve systemwide, systematic change to help people in an organization work more effectively in achieving organizational goals (whatever that means). We were learning, and there was much to learn. It was indeed an exciting time to be a management trainer and a management consultant.

In the 1990s, we have arrived at a point at which we know a great deal of what we need to know about how people behave at work, what turns them on, what makes them productive, what makes them work well and happily, what gives them satisfaction. Are we training managers to understand and to use this knowledge? I don't think so—certainly not universally. There may be a number of reasons for this, but I'll offer only two at the outset that may be considered harsh. I think that too many trainers have been running training departments instead of helping to run companies. I also believe that many managers have abdicated their responsibility to manage the training and development of their people.

I continue to hear nonsense about management training. For example, it is still often spoken of as "soft stuff," as contrasted with the supposedly harder technical skills training. There is nothing soft about the knowledge we have about how to manage. People such as Argyris, Maslow, Herzberg, McGregor, Vroom, Likert, Blake and Mouton, and countless others have given us the empirical data we need to do a good job. It's about as hard as we could hope for.

I also hear HRD professionals complaining that managers are too obsessed with short-term results to do the long-term work of developing their subordinates. My response is that we trainers obviously have done a very poor job of convincing managers that they can get almost immediate results from the training we can give their subordinates. You can't get much more short-term than immediate.

## Conclusion

This book is about partnerships. It's about how human resource professionals and functioning managers can work together to get the kinds of results they can get and should want. And those results all lead to the same ends: superior management and committed employees.

You can well imagine that in thirty years one can accumulate all sorts of conceits and biases. Many of mine are collected here, and I take responsibility for them. The wonderful thing about dealing with biases is that I have no problem with your freedom to do whatever you like with them. You may accept them in whole or in part; you may quarrel with them and question them. That's fine. Recently, following one of my presentations to trainers, one person wrote on the evaluation sheet, "He thinks he's a curmudgeon but actually he's an arrogant, insufferable bore!" Well, I guess there are times when I am curmudgeonly. Probably I've also come across at times as arrogant, and heaven knows I have on occasion been insufferable (I'm grateful for good friends who have not deserted me, notwithstanding). But it would disturb me to bore you. So I hope you will find my biases thought provoking rather than boring.

## Acknowledgment

I interviewed a number of experienced training professionals, chiefly during April of 1989, when I was yet unsure of the form this book would take. I've listed their names in Chapter Two. I want them to know that I am deeply grateful to them for their help and candor.

*New York, New York*                                    Thomas L. Quick
*March 1991*

*To Vicki Robin*

# ■ The Author ■

THOMAS L. QUICK entered the executive and management development field in 1961, when he joined the Research Institute of America as a salesman for the institute's self-development programs for
executives, salespeople, and supervisors. In 1966, he joined the institute's professional staff, where he rose to the position of directing
editor, supervising the staffs of the newsletters that constituted the
sales and management membership programs. He left RIA in 1982
to help form the Resource Strategies Institute. As executive director,
he edits its two monthly newsletters, *Professional Managing* and
*Professional Selling*.

Drawing on his experience as both a line manager and a
salesman, Quick has written more than twenty books. His interviews and articles, numbering more than 500, have appeared in
magazines and journals such as *Working Woman, Cosmopolitan,
Success, Boardroom Reports, Training, Training and Development
Journal, Trainer's Workshop, Creative Management,* and others.
His monthly column in *Training News* won the Dugan Laird
award for distinguished writing on human resources. Currently, he
is a columnist for the American Public Radio program "Market-
place" and for *Sales and Marketing Management* magazine.

Quick maintains an active practice in training and organization development consulting in New York City and California. He served two terms as president of the New York Metro chapter of the American Society for Training and Development and one term as Region One director for national ASTD.

# Training Managers
## *So They Can*
# Really Manage

# PART ONE

# What's Wrong
# with Management Training?

American corporations will spend approximately $10 billion this year to train their supervisors and managers to manage subordinates effectively, that is, to get the results from employees' efforts that the organizations want. (That's the figure given me by Anthony P. Carnevale, vice-president of the American Society for Training and Development.) Much of that money will be wasted. And it will be wasted needlessly.

Trainees will sit in classrooms and training courses and listen to multitudes of management theories, concepts, principles, and techniques. But there will be shockingly little learning, considering the enormous investment of money and time (I have no way to estimate the dollars involved in lost performance time away from work). The root of the problem is in our failure to understand how adults learn.

First, adult learners must see a reason for learning, one that they consider valuable. But often, supervisors and managers are enrolled in programs they consider irrelevant, or impractical, or not believable. Their bosses have not provided the essential linkage of classroom to workplace, and the trainers also do not provide this link and are seen as not credible, not plugged in to the functional areas of the organization. The trainees may see the content of the course as too generic or theoretical. Thus from the outset the trainees may see little relationship between what they hear in the classroom and what they must do on the job. They may see little value in the training; thus there probably is very little learning.

Second, once they are back on the job, the trainees may be unable or unwilling to try to apply what was given them in the classroom. The day-to-day demands of the job, the firefighting, may squeeze out the opportunities to apply the new techniques and knowledge. Or the newly returned managers may be at a loss to know when and how to practice their new learning, because their bosses don't provide guidance through coaching or mentoring. If the trainees sense that what they've absorbed in the classroom goes against the culture of the department or of the organization as a whole, or it seems to run counter to their bosses' style, they'll be unwilling to take the risk of application.

The enemy of learning is the retention curve. As it dips, people forget. If the trainees don't have the chance or neglect to apply the new knowledge, they begin to lose it. Probably most of the course content is gone by the end of three months unless there is a conscious effort to remember it, and without practice, much of the experience will remain a classroom exercise.

There are two other components of adult learning, feedback and rewards. As the managers apply the new knowledge, they need feedback on how well or inadequately they are applying it. If they need help in correcting, they should receive that as quickly after the application as possible. If the application of the new knowledge is successful, they need to have that reinforced by positive feedback. Again, the praise or other reward must be given as soon after the application as possible, so that the experience is fresh in the manager's mind and so that he or she has a clear idea of what is to be repeated. Through the repetition, of course, the learning takes root. In my thirty years of management experience, training as well as performing, I've heard consistently that most managers do not do well at giving feedback to subordinates on their performance. Their subordinates have told me; the managers themselves have admitted it.

In time, the training is dismissed by the managers and their managers. Too bad. Perhaps it might have been valuable and workable under different circumstances. But doubtless the circumstances don't change, and future training investments have to be written off as pure cost. In time, everyone gets a bit cynical about the value of training. It's far from unusual for a trainer to feel a wall of resistance as he or she starts a program. The trainees are saying to themselves, "It hasn't worked before. Why should we believe it will this time?" Sometimes they even voice that thought to the trainer.

# ■ 1 ■

# The Failure to Produce
# Effective Managers

Although my thirty years of experience in the training and development field have given me a certain authority and credibility, still I'm obliged, I think, to present some objective evidence of our failure to produce managers who are effective.

*Item.* Fewer than 25 percent of employees in this country believe they are well managed. That's the dismal conclusion of a study done by the consulting firm the Hay Group: *Linking New Employee Attitudes and Values to Improved Productivity, Cost, and Quality* (1989). The report also states that three out of four employees believe their companies are doing a poor job of retaining high-quality employees. Gresham's law of management says that poor managers drive out the good. Most employees say that their companies don't treat them with respect. Incidentally, the Hay Group has shown these results in studies before; these facts are not just now making their appearance.

*Item.* Management consultant John F. Budd, Jr., quoting a survey done by researchers at Carnegie-Mellon University, wrote in the *Wall Street Journal* in the spring of 1990 that more than half of the managers questioned say they don't believe top management. One-third don't even trust their immediate bosses.

*Item.* High-level management is to blame when quality is low, again according to a survey quoted in a July 1990 issue of the

*Wall Street Journal.* This time the study was done by consultants of Brooks International. Top executives may say they are committed to high quality standards, but only about half of their middle managers believe they are, and even fewer supervisors and rank-and-filers find top management credible.

*Item.* Apparently W. Edwards Deming, the famous American consultant who has done so much over the past forty years to help Japanese concerns achieve high quality standards, would not be surprised by the Brooks study. Deming was interviewed by the *Wall Street Journal* for its June 4, 1990, issue about what is wrong with American corporations. Among his replies was, "We are all born with intrinsic motivation, self-esteem, dignity, an eagerness to learn. Our present system of management crushes that all out." He believes that competition, not cooperation, characterizes many American business corporations: "All people ask for is a chance to work with pride and joy. Management has taken all of it out. Then you take quality out. Instead of working for the company, people compete with each other."

*Item.* The M.I.T. Commission on Industrial Productivity, in a book that its members—economists, scientists, engineers, management specialists—produced (*Made in America,* 1990), castigates management for its preoccupation with short-term results, outdated strategies, and dissipation of our most precious resource, people. As is the case with Deming, these folks are pessimistic about our future as a player in global wealth and power.

*Item.* In 1983, the nonprofit Public Agenda Foundation of New York released a study on the work ethic in which they stated that only 22 percent of American workers believe there is a direct relationship between how hard they work and how much they are paid. The more recent Hay Group survey, noted above, also found that many people fail to see that their performance influences their rewards. Ironically, monetary rewards have traditionally been touted by American management as what Americans primarily work for, yet management seem to be quite indifferent to the value of those rewards. In all these years of management training and development, we have apparently failed to establish fundamental truths in our trainees. For the record, I do not agree with many managers that money is the most important thing to workers. In any survey of employees' values, money is fourth or fifth on the list. Opportunity, challenge, and interesting work are usually reported as more important.

## Where's the Progress?

These figures hold no surprises for me, and I seriously doubt that they would come as a revelation to most people who are in the business of training managers. Most of my colleagues with whom I have talked in the years in which I have been active in ASTD and the training community readily acknowledge that there have been substantial shortfalls in our efforts to upgrade the quality of American management. In fact, for this book I interviewed more than twenty experienced trainers who were recommended to me as top people, and one of my questions dealt with the failure of traditional training and development (T&D) approaches to produce effective managers. Their agreement on the failure was virtually unanimous. What these approaches are and why they haven't been successful are described in Chapter Two.

Meanwhile, we continue to train supervisors and managers who then return to their employees and often revert to the same destructive and obstructive behaviors they practiced before. They threaten. They punish arbitrarily. They shut their people out of any goal-setting. They're capricious in appraising. They withhold feedback. They pounce on mistakes. They yell at employees and humiliate them. They refuse to trust subordinates. They create tension and competition and sow distrust among subordinates. They don't begin to understand how to reward good performance. And they don't listen.

Those are just a few of the minor faults that employees complain about. If you've worked in organizational life for even a short time, you have your own war stories. I remember my own experience at the company I loved for so long, the Research Institute of America. After giving sound, enlightened advice to our subscribers for thirty years, we suffered a change of management. We went from an open system to one that closed tightly. In the old days, communications flowed freely, up, down, sideways, and, just as important, inside-outside. Some of our bosses were not very good managers, but they usually stayed out of the way. They knew how to hire bright, creative people and give them a lot of room. If you didn't like what was going on, you thought nothing of letting higher management know. If you had a question about any part of the operation, you could go to anyone from the president on down. I didn't always agree with the varying styles of management, but, while complaining, I went ahead, as others did, and did my own thing the way I wanted to do it. Some of my friends in other companies had better expense accounts, traveled perhaps to more exotic places, made more money, had nicer titles, but I had the one thing that was most important to me: freedom to, as Maslow said, actualize myself, to be what I could be.

In the 1970s, after many years of advising tens of thousands of managers in every part of the country and in every kind of business, we had new management. Top management made it very clear that they didn't trust us. The president spent a lot of time and uttered a lot of profanity trying to discover who leaked information to the rest of us. Although many of us were considered by our subscribers to be experts in our field, some had advanced degrees, some had been valued members of the professional staff, we were treated as children.

Perhaps the best way to illustrate the new atmosphere is with a memo from one of the directing editors, following up an astonishing letter to all of us advising that we were expected to be at our desks at nine in the morning, to take an hour for lunch (unless we were hosting and interviewing), and to stay until five.

Here's the follow-up memo that made most of us feel that we now were employed by a company very different from the one we had enjoyed and worked hard for:

Subject: Working Hours

The memo from ——— of the 26th relative to work hours is clear and not subject to reinterpretation. However, several of you have asked such things as "What if my train is late?" or "What if I come in early regularly?" etc. Here's how I read the 9 to 5, 5-day-a-week requirement:
1. Habitual tardiness will not be tolerated. An occasional late train, traffic jam, subway snarl—these cannot be anticipated, and I have not in the past and will not in the future get excited over unavoidable occurrences. But the accent here is on "occasional," which means that if you have to get

started earlier to get to work on time regularly, then that is what you have to do.

2. If you choose to be at your desk earlier than 9 A.M., or work through lunch hour, or stay after 5 P.M., such deviations from the 9 to 5 requirement (with the normal hour off for lunch) are by your option.

3. I cannot foresee any circumstance where there will be an undeniable business advantage in working at home. We've had no problem with this in the past; but, for the record, presence in the office is required every day of the full workweek.

You can see from the foregoing that I intend to enforce the 9 to 5, 5-day-a-week requirement in the strictest possible fashion. The need for such strict enforcement across-the-board should be obvious to all. Otherwise, specific exceptions will inevitably and gradually lead to the sort of violations which the October 26th memo from ———— was intended to correct.

At that point, we all knew we worked for a company in decline. The company, incidentally, no longer exists. It is hard for me to imagine saying such things to people in their forties, fifties, and sixties, many of whom had national reputations. I strongly suspect, however, that most people working in most organizations today would not find such a memo to be strange.

What has distressed me for a long time is that, in my seminars and workshops, I find managers expressing essentially the same concerns and asking the same questions I have heard for the better part of three decades. Their organizations have spent tons of money on training, and the industry has spawned legions of trainers and consultants. Why have we had so little effect?

*Setting Goals: A Rare Practice.* Let's take the important function of setting goals as an illustration of how little progress we've made. It is inconceivable to me that a manager could hope to enlist the commitment and enhance the motivation of his or her people to achieve organizational goals if the manager does not share those goals—and his or her performance standards—with subordinates. Yet we know that most managers do not periodically sit down with employees to explain goals toward which they want subordinates to work. Year after year most employees work rather blindly. They don't know the targets at which they are supposed to aim.

When I talk with managers, I ask for a show of hands to indicate whether they regularly and periodically do this. A few hands may go up. When I talk with corporate trainers, I ask them how many work with managers who regularly set goals and explain standards to their people. Only a few hands go up. "Why do you suppose they don't?" I ask. Some of the trainers' answers: "They don't know the goals themselves." "They're too busy putting out fires." "They assume their employees already know the goals." And one of my favorites: "They don't want to have to talk with their subordinates." They don't want to have to listen to them, either.

In my motivation seminars, I ask managers to respond to these ten statements as honestly as they can:

1.  I try to have goal-setting sessions at least once a year with all my employees.
2.  When possible, I ask them to join with me in setting worthwhile goals for the department.
3.  With employees whose performance is reliable, I often leave it to them to determine the methods they will use to reach their goals.
4.  I invite employees to set personal goals for their growth and advancement.
5.  I try to know what employees want out of their work and what their needs and goals are.
6.  Once I have agreed on a goal, I make sure it is accounted for.
7.  I let employees know at the time of setting goals how important they are to me.
8.  I usually incorporate goals in appraisals.
9.  I make sure to find out how realistic the goals seem to employees who are charged with reaching them.
10. I make sure that all employees periodically understand not only my goals but the performance standards I expect of them.

If you can agree with all of the above statements, you're exceptional. I doubt whether most managers today can agree with the majority of them. In one recent seminar, one of the participants surprised and delighted me by saying that he agreed with all ten statements. I complimented him highly. A few minutes later, either he understood what he had not previously or his conscience bothered him. He interrupted me: "Tom, I agreed with all ten statements not because I do these things. I don't. But I believe they should be done."

I ask again, how can managers hope to run their departments, plan the work, and get everyone to go in the same direction unless they periodically and regularly explain goals and standards to their subordinates and enlist them in the departmental effort to practice the standards and achieve the goals? That to me is Management 101.

*The Importance of Motivation.* It is in the area of motivation of people at work that I see the greatest failings. Most training programs seem to give very little emphasis to the subject. Through the years I've surveyed trainers about how they present motivation, and in my interviews with top trainers for this book, I asked them how they train their managers in the area of motivation. The following are representative of the answers I get:

*Motivation is a subset.* The subject of motivation is usually presented as a part of another module, such as leadership or improving productivity or interpersonal skills. One top trainer told me that he doubted whether motivation could be delivered as a separate subject.

*Motivation training is generic and eclectic.* Some trainers describe their programs as a review of the various motivation theories. They are somewhat vague about how the generic or eclectic review is linked to the real problems managers face on the job. I've never forgotten my own experience with a highly theoretical presentation on motivation back in the late 1960s at the University of Michigan. After the professor who taught this segment of the program for managers described "his" theory of motivation, I asked him: "How would the manager actually put theory into practice?" "I don't know," he replied. I don't think I remembered the theory one day later.

*There is heavy concentration on Maslow and Herzberg.* Later in this book I deal with the theories of these two social scientists more in depth, as well as with my objections to using them as the basis for motivation training. For the moment, I'll simply say that I have never known how to train managers to use Maslow's hierarchy of needs, and although I find Herzberg's two-factor theory helpful, the ambiguities in it are troublesome. I tend to use Herzberg to bolster Expectancy Theory, which in my experience is more practical. Before a full discussion of Expectancy Theory, however, let me assert that there is no more important subject in management training and development than the motivation of people at work. In fact, in Chapter Five you will read my argument that almost all of management training should be presented in the context of motivation. Motivation is the book, not the chapter. It is the essence of managing people. Unless employees are motivated to do a good job, unless they commit themselves to achieving the organizational goals, how can anyone reasonably expect anything but, at best, mediocre productivity from them?

The manager is the key to stimulating motivation in employees. It is the manager who persuades employees that his or her goals are important to them. It is the manager who makes the work valuable to employees. It is the manager who gives them feedback as they try to do the work. And finally, it is the manager who recognizes, reinforces, and rewards the good work, the achievement of the organizational goals. Virtually every contact a manager has with subordinates has a potential impact, positively or negatively, on their motivation. Whether over time people give a damn about what they do and how they do it in very large part depends on the person to whom they report.

Yet how do many of us study motivation? With a review of the theories? As a few hours at most in another training module? By using a theory that has little or no practical value? What's the message that we then broadcast loudly and clearly to managers? Don't worry about motivation. It isn't all that important. How that kind of message can be delivered after decades of important research into the behavior of people at work I cannot imagine. But what I do know is that there are millions of employees out there who would like to do a good job, because it's important to them, if only their managers would give them the means to do that job.

### Expectancy Theory

I often say that Expectancy Theory has to be one of the best kept management secrets of our time. Most managers have never heard of it. Many trainers know little or nothing about it, and of those who do, few use it as the basis for training managers to manage the motivation of their people, clearly the most important task they have. By the very definition of the term, a manager gets things done through others.

The great psychologist Kurt Lewin, who fled Hitler's Germany to come to the United States early in the 1930s, was fond of saying, "There is nothing so practical as a good theory." Expectancy Theory, which everyone should know, is a practical theory. It is mainstream psychology that has been around for a long time. It is simple (so much so that some people may suspect that it doesn't work), and it does work.

Human behavior, the theory holds, is a function of (1) the value of the reward that people may expect to gain as a result of a particular choice of action or a decision and (2) the expectation that they can enjoy the reward without undue risk or hardship. People will do what they feel most rewarded for doing, as long as they think they can be successful in getting the reward without taking too many chances or stretching themselves excessively. Most people are not high on risk taking. If you want to influence someone to do something, make it sufficiently valuable to the person and provide whatever help and encouragement are necessary for the person to feel confident about doing what you want. (This subject is covered at greater length in Chapter Five.)

Building on this theory, which applies to everyone in every situation (psychotic behavior excepted), there are five practical steps for the manager, covering his or her dealings with subordinates:

1. Tell employees what you expect them to do—your goals and standards.
2. Make the work valuable to employees, chiefly by assigning them to work they like and can do well. If they achieve personal goals and satisfaction from helping you, they're committed people.
3. Make the work doable by giving them the resources they need to be successful—training, coaching, mentoring, equipment, and so on.

4.  While they are trying to do what you want, give them feedback on how they are doing—correct mistakes, reinforce success.
5.  When they have done what you want, reward them. Praise will do just fine.

As you'll see later in the book, these five steps cover just about everything a manager does.

### Assessing Your Managers

How much skill and knowledge do your supervisors and managers display in managing the motivation of their subordinates? Following are some statements relating to their managing. Thinking of your people, would you agree with them? The number to the right of each question is the score you receive for each affirmative response. (No score for negative responses.)

1.  They sometimes complain about the unmotivated people in their departments.                                                          −1
2.  Their appraisals of their employees reflect their concern for the growth and development of their employees.         +1
3.  They regularly and periodically sit down with their key people to coach them on how to make themselves more valuable to the organization.                       +1
4.  They complain about having to appraise the performance of their subordinates.                                                    −1
5.  They believe that you shouldn't have to reward an employee for doing what he or she is supposed to do.              −1
6.  They complain that too many employees want to know what's in it for them before taking on additional responsibility.                                                           −1
7.  They frequently tell you what employees say to them about organizational policy, management strategy, and ideas for improving the operation.                              +1
8.  They believe that an important part of the manager's job is to motivate his or her subordinates.                            −1

9. You hear from them periodically about the superior performance of their more valuable employees. +1
10. They believe that the best way to get good performance is to be nice to employees. −1
11. They say that you cannot afford to be nice to some employees because those subordinates will take advantage of you. −1
12. They are reluctant to criticize employees' performance because they say it tends to reduce morale and create resistance. −1
13. They complain periodically that many employees don't seem to take their work as seriously as they should. −1
14. They press you for higher pay increases for their employees who perform exceptionally well. +1
15. They grouse about the fact that employees are increasingly unwilling to put in a fair day's work for a fair day's pay. −1
16. Their style of managing poor performers reflects their confidence that almost every employee's deficient performance can be turned around. +1
17. Their initial reaction when mistakes occur is to assign blame. −1
18. They regularly invite their subordinates to help them make decisions that will affect those employees. +1
19. Sometimes you hear accurate information about your managers' departments and employees before you hear it from the managers. −1
20. In your conversations with your managers' employees, you get a strong sense that they always know what departmental goals are and their part in achieving them. +1
21. They are careful to protect their managerial prerogatives. −1
22. They sometimes discount information they receive from employees about the operation on the grounds that the employees aren't able to grasp the big picture or don't know enough about the operation. −1

23. They often publicize the accomplishments of their key
subordinates throughout their departments and to you.     +1
24. When they discuss their most valuable employees with
you, you know that their approval is based primarily
on the employees' performance.                            +1
25. When employee performance is disappointing, your
managers tend to pinpoint causes outside of themselves,
such as poor work ethic or company policies or
setbacks.                                                 −1
26. They express their belief that most employees do not
want criticism.                                           −1
27. It is not unusual for your managers to complain
that they don't have enough money to motivate their
people properly.                                          −1
28. You sense that many employees who report to your
managers do what they feel they must to get by and
not much more.                                            −1
29. They believe that they draw much of their power
from the demonstrated competence of their employees.      +1
30. They generally express their conviction that the vast
majority of employees genuinely want to do a good job.    +1

A perfect score is 12. Did you find to your satisfaction that
all of your managers do everything right? Good for you. However,
I suspect that most managers honestly responding to all thirty statements might arrive at much lower scores, even some negative ones.
Let us go over the statements that have negative score points.

1. There are no unmotivated people. These managers are
telling you they can't get people to do what they want.

4. They complain because they don't know how to appraise
or they worry about being fair or having to reveal that they have
problems with some employees. It's also likely that they see appraisals as negative, that is, primarily criticism, rather than action plans
that point to better performance.

5. People do what they feel rewarded for doing. If you withhold rewards when I work well for you, I'm likely not to continue
to work well. Forget about the annual merit increase or my pay in
general. It's not much of a motivator—or a reward.

6. Of course they want to know why they should do it, or why they should want to do it. That's true of all of us. These managers aren't taking the time to show their people why.

8. Motivation is not something you do to someone. Motivation comes from within. The manager provides the reward for the motivating forces in the employees.

10. Who says? Being nice is nice, but providing clear direction and rewarding good performance are better. Niceness is gravy.

11. No alert manager will let an employee take advantage for long, or even for the second time.

12. If they don't do it right, it surely will.

13. These managers fail to get the seriousness across.

15. Perhaps they should try giving other rewards, such as praise. When people feel appreciated, they perk up.

17. Their first reaction ought to be to find a solution or a correction.

19. You have to ask yourself why your managers are slow to give you feedback.

21. This means they probably are not delegating or letting go of work they should be pushing down. Why are they reluctant?

22. Chances are the employees know more about their part of the operation than the managers, who aren't willing to admit it.

25. Try talking to the employees about the poor performance, and they'll probably point to the manager as a big problem. Poor performance in a department can usually be traced to poor management.

26. Most employees want to do a good job, and if helpful criticism keeps them from floundering or failing, they welcome it. These managers are trying to avoid a painful but necessary job.

27. No doubt the employees know and accept that reality. Encourage these managers to be creative in finding nonmonetary ways to reward good performance.

28. This indicates possibly serious motivation problems that your managers are not identifying and correcting.

Now that you've thought about it more, how many of your responses would you change?

## What Makes a Good Meeting?

If you still waver in accepting my premise that we haven't done a good job overall in training and developing our managers to be more effective, let me move away from the more complex areas of managing to an ever present example of inadequacy in leadership: the common, garden-variety meeting. Many people in organizations say they spend (waste?) anywhere from one-third to one-half of their working time in meetings. And if you are an outsider trying to contact someone on the inside, you may be tempted to believe that many people spend all their time in the conference room or the boss's office.

Surely in the last three decades we have learned everything there is to know about how to run an effective meeting, by which I mean one that has objectives that are clear to everyone and accomplishes its business in a reasonable period of time. In a good meeting, one can observe the following: People arrive promptly with an understanding of what the meeting is about. There is a lively discussion of the issues with everyone not only respecting the rights of others to talk but also actively encouraging full contributions. Everyone is supportive of all, even when they don't agree with others' opinions or conclusions. Leadership passes around the table freely as certain people step in to exercise their authority in certain areas. The discussion continues until every possible option is explored and a decision is then made by consensus. Everyone leaves the room stimulated by the deliberation and believing that the decision they've reached is probably the best one they could have. Everyone is therefore committed to seeing the decision carried out. The meeting has taken no more than ninety minutes.

How many such meetings have you attended lately? They're not very common. You'll instead see people trying to dominate the discussion and keep others from having much say. There is a lot of interrupting and ignoring people's comments. There is impatience to have an early vote rather than to keep the table open to every possible option. The meeting drags on; tempers fray and impatience grows. Rear ends become numb from having sat too long in one place. People leave the meeting with misgivings that they might have to make the decision all over again in a couple of days.

We should be training everyone in the dynamics of good meeting leadership, but I doubt that we are, judging from most of the meetings I attend. I am especially discouraged when I see trainers, who are supposed to be training others in good meeting management, run poor meetings and make all the mistakes that untrained people do.

So, I rest my case. Surely, now that you've been provoked by my perceptions and biases, you are rethinking your original reactions that of course your people have been well trained and continually developed on the job. I have no doubt that you are seeing a number of areas in which there could be solid improvement. In Chapter Two, you'll see how some very experienced trainers see the failures of some of the traditional methods we have resorted to through the years to make better managers. In subsequent chapters you will have an opportunity to evaluate my suggestions for you, the manager, and you, the trainer, to work together to achieve more creditable results in developing managers who are good at managing people.

# ■ 2 ■

# Professionals Speak Out
# About Training Practices

I've always believed that in management training and development there has been a conspiracy of silence. Management wasn't eager to acknowledge that its multibillion-dollar investment in producing more effective managers hadn't justified itself with impressive dividends. And we trainers hardly wanted to publicize our expensive failures. "I won't talk about it if you won't talk about it."

In this chapter, my colleagues and I do talk about it. So much for the conspiracy theory. And I cherish the hope that my managerial colleagues will become increasingly emboldened to go public with their frustrations, puzzlement, and disappointments over the glaring lack of success in the past three decades in creating managers who affirm the American myth—that we have the best.

In the spring of 1989, with the help of a number of HRD people who were active in ASTD, I compiled a list of more than twenty training professionals who, by any reasonable standards, could be considered successful and at the top of their profession. In each telephone interview, I started out with the statement, "Many of us in this field do not believe that management training and development in this country have been as effective as they ought to have been." I was not astonished when virtually all of them unhesitatingly agreed that our results have been considerably less than spectacular. I followed this premise with two questions: "What are some of the practices of the past that have proved ineffective?" "What's your opinion of management skills training?" The latter has to do with familiar current practices in delivering such skills training.

To a person, they were candid and quite forthcoming, as you'll see. Each segment begins with a quote from one of those whom I interviewed. As a manager, how many of these practices and deficiencies can you recognize in the training programs you send your supervisors and managers to? (Incidentally, I don't think the trainers interviewed should be held accountable for the editorializing that follows their contributions. That is my doing.)

*Trainers say, "We've only got them for three days. Let's give them everything we can."*

Nancy K. McGee
Vice-President
C&S Georgia Corporation

A few years ago, I chuckled over an article in the *Wall Street Journal* written by a befuddled manager who had just returned from six weeks of management training—obviously one of those comprehensive courses. His complaint was not with the thoroughness of the program—quite the opposite. He felt he had received too much; he couldn't remember which solution went with which problem. It was an information overload. Nancy McGee went on to say that she believed the training is more helpful when it is spaced out and focuses on specific skills.

She expressed a temptation that is all too common. Companies have asked me to conduct one-day seminars in the management of motivation. My last book on the subject—*The Manager's Motivation Desk Book* (1985)—contained 454 pages of text, all directed to the manager. You want me to cover everything in one day? Yes, you say, that's all the money and time we have for this. You want me to "give them everything"? I shall, but I have no illusions that much learning will take place. The trainees will take home a full notebook, which many of them will never look at again. There's so much to try to remember that it becomes intimidating. Actually, as you'll see in Chapter Five, I advocate presenting motivation as the context for most management training, with the various subsidiary modules being delivered over time, not all at once.

*Trainees are brought into a classroom, get excited, then return to an environment that doesn't always match what they've been taught.*

Margaret M. O'Donnell
Manager of Training and Development
Minnesota Mutual Life Insurance Company

Margaret O'Donnell comments that many trainees learn in a safe environment, one that isn't necessarily connected to the company or department culture. What I say to trainees at the beginning of a program is, "The sooner these walls come down, the sooner we'll see some real learning." The classroom should not be an artificial environment—the walls come down to permit real-life, real-time training. But there is often an unwitting conspiracy between trainers and trainees to avoid dealing with cultures outside the room. The problems back on the job, and the people who cause or foster them, are simply too threatening.

Two examples from my own experience come readily to mind. One involved a rather standard three-day program for the middle managers of the company where I was employed. A new trainer was brought on board, and she immediately began to interview all of us who would be attending the program. She heard a lot of disturbing things about the company: almost no communication, almost no trust, almost no morale. Middle managers were floundering in their attempts to hold their operations together, with no perceived help from top management. From the outset of the three days, it was obvious to all of us that no serious problems would be addressed. It was very safe content, such as how to listen, time management, analytical skills. The interpersonal and leadership problems that some of us saw as destroying the company were totally ignored—they were simply too threatening. We didn't bring them up. Neither did she. Everyone pretended. It was an enjoyable three days in an expensive hotel, with lots of good food and booze.

The other example occurred in the late 1960s during a two-week program of sensitivity training, which is largely an unstructured group experience in which the participants hope to learn to deal with their own and others' (usually strangers') problems in a group setting. I watched all of us create a friendly environment. We became chummy and affectionate and collegial. It was a love fest. But it bore almost no relationship to the outside world. When I returned to that outside world that was not chummy and congenial and collegial, I suffered severe reentry problems, and I'm sure that most others did as well. It was a distinctly painful experience. More than twenty years later, I can recall it vividly.

That's not an experience we want our trainees to have. In the above two instances, what some of us took back to the work scene were major frustration and hurt.

*There is often a lack of senior management sponsorship.*
Sue Thompson
Director, Human Resource Development
Levi Strauss & Company

I can verify that this deplorable situation does not exist at Levi Strauss. A few years back, I interviewed Sue Thompson about their "Quality Enhancement" effort, an employee involvement program. The administrators of the program were proceeding slowly, training from the top down, to create a supportive structure for quality circles. In the early days, many corporations, attracted to the idea of quality circles, found them disappointing and short-lived, largely because they hadn't created the base of management support. Managers perceived the employee circles as threats to their power and authority.

Dr. Scott Parry, chairman of Training House, Inc., comments that in many organizations training is sponsored by the corporate education or training department rather than by management. And when training is (in the words of Badi G. Foster, president of the Aetna Institute for Corporate Education at Aetna Life and Casualty Company) "instructor-driven rather than learner-driven," it is "disconnected from the strategic thinking" of the company. Then you're likely to find what Scott Parry calls "the annual sheep-dip. Everyone in," whether you need it or not.

The lack of senior management sponsorship also carries the message that it's not really important, or that there is something wrong with the trainees that needs to be fixed but nothing wrong with top management. In the case of the three-day safe seminar that I attended and described above, the chairman of the board sat through most sessions but declined to participate in the discussions or exercises. His nonverbal communication: "This is for you, not us." Actually, the truth was even less pleasant. Later, someone asked the human resource director, who initiated the training, whether there would be similar programs for the people at the top. "Oh, no," he said, "they would be too threatened."

I should add that I was barred from further management training sessions because of my severely negative evaluation of the trainer and the training.

*Much management training is intermittent and one-shot.*
                                        Stein A. Roaldset
                                             President
        Scandinavian Management Development Corporation


Stein Roaldset typifies a certain attitude toward training with this quotation, very much like what he has heard from American trainers and managers: "We did management training three years ago. It's too soon to do it again." It sounds incredible, but Stein Roaldset gets support from other interviewees. Marianne Matheis, head of training and development at The Aerospace Corporation, believes that most training is a periodic event, without much reinforcement. A third voice is that of Dr. R. Ronald Shepps, manager of training and development at Harley-Davidson, Inc., who sees a widespread failure in companies to follow up and to provide refresher training. Training is insufficient over time, in and out.

One extremely regrettable result of the intermittency, the lack of continuity, is segmentation. As Roaldset points out, every skill presented is separate. The modules are, as Badi Foster says, segmented and fragmented learning events. Here's a real management program of twenty-four modules developed by an insurance company:

Part One:
Working with the Individual

1. Coaching
2. Delegating
3. Counseling
4. Constructive Feedback
5. Performance Problems
6. New Employee Orientation
7. Performance Appraisal
8. Employee Development

Part Two:
Working with Employees as a Group

9. Recruiting, Selecting, Hiring
10. The Learning Process
11. Organizing a Training Program
12. Planning and Conducting Meetings
13. Developing Leadership Skills
14. Maintaining Control of a Workforce
15. Motivating and Stimulating People

Part Three:
Developing Your Administrative and Executive Skills

16. Self-Assessment and Development
17. Thinking Creatively
18. Solving Problems and Making Decisions
19. Negotiating
10. Increasing Your Administrative Efficiency
21. Improving Communication Skills
22. Effective Written Communication
23. Understanding Business Economics and Accounting
24. Developing a Top-Management Point of View

Very complete. But why in this particular order? And doesn't communication have something to do with other people? So, why is it in Part Three? Why does Employee Orientation follow Performance Problems in Part One? Why, again in Part One, does Employee Development trail behind all the modules such as Delegating, Coaching, Performance Appraisal, and so on?

What's the inner logic to this sequence of development? I can't see it. What does it all add up to? A certificate, most likely, evidence of having completed all the twenty-four modules. Whoopee! It appears to satisfy the educator's desire to be sure to cover everything. That takes care of the instructor's needs, but what about the learner's needs: to have some purpose, some context, some system. Beautiful designs are inputs. The learner needs outputs, through being able to apply the new knowledge. The reason for the coaching, counseling, feedback, delegating, appraisal, and so on follows them all. It makes tremendous sense.

*The model of school prevails.*

Don Begosh
Director of Personnel Development
and Planning
Lever Brothers Company

Indeed. The above segment demonstrates one aspect of this tendency to duplicate the educational classroom. Don Begosh observes that people need experience to develop skills. They don't learn simply by sitting in a classroom listening to someone lecture. Dr. Richard P. Kropp, Jr., director of human resource development at Wang Laboratories, Inc. at the time of the interview and now associate professor at the University of Massachusetts, believes that management development must move out of the classroom. Kropp echoes what John Murphy, then director (and now president of his own firm) of executive education at GTE, said to me several years ago: "When you're consolidating training in a center" (as his company did), "the training professional must climb over the wall and go to where the problems are."

The problem is that many trainers, having come from academia, seem to be convinced that the real action takes place in the classroom. In the classroom, it is easy for trainers to distance themselves from the realities of the business and to say, as Sue Thompson charges, "We do not hold ourselves accountable to the bottom line."

Management training should be more than textbooks and

theories, says Carol Phillips, vice-president, quality resource manager at C&S/Sovran Corporation. And yet many trainers are seduced
by the elaborateness of the classroom presentation: slides, movies,
interactive video, role plays, case studies, audiotapes and videotapes,
overheads, well-filled flipcharts. But that's all preliminary stuff.
Carol Phillips is correct when she says, "Front line realities make
better managers." You must provide more experiential training for
supervisors and managers.

Another aspect of the classroom can be a drawback: the
parent-to-child transaction that Scott Parry believes can characterize
much of the transfer of knowledge. Trainers who stand before a
group and sense their power to control what goes on may not remember that the transfer of knowledge in the training group is three
way: instructor to trainees, trainees to trainees, and trainees to
instructor.

> *Management training can become too standardized. One size
> fits all.*
>
> Scott Parry, Ph.D.
> Chairman
> Training House, Inc.

Scott Parry is fond of using biblical language to describe the
annual sheep-dip: "And a levy went out to all the world." Don
Begosh of Lever Brothers talks about the perception that "corporate
development can produce managers like we produce detergents at
the end of a packaging line." And Mal Warren, vice-president, staffing and development at CVS, criticizes generic curricula. One size
fits all.

Once again, this is the school model. Everyone takes the same
thing at the same speed, regardless of whether you need "special ed"
or the classroom model. The answer is to develop an individual
development program for each learner, but that really must be done
with the learner's boss.

My former employer resorted to the one-size approach to a
ridiculous extreme. Some of us who attended had been preparing
self-learning programs for managers for years, and yet we were ex-

pected to sit in for three days exposed to the same content as every other manager in our company, most of whom did not have the sophistication that we on the professional staff possessed. We were thus spending a lot of time to learn little. Had the program been tailored to our needs, the other managers would have been at a disadvantage. In addition, the message that the professionals received was that our work was perceived by management as not important.

It's well to keep in mind that training programs can carry negative messages with them. They can be condescending, in which case they discount the trainees. Or they can be boring, in which case the learners resent the waste of time.

*Management training is forced on people. They need to want development.*

Murray Blank
Director
Management and Organization Development
Bell Atlantic

We should do an individual needs assessment. Providing training without it is prescribing before diagnosing, says Murray Blank (now internal consultant at Baltimore Gas & Electric). "What do you want to do differently?" is a question Al Versacci, vice-president of corporate training at Amerada Hess Corporation, finds useful to ask. In that way, trainees have a chance to buy into the program, and the program itself is more focused and relevant for them. The questions Richard S. D. Hawkins, manager of management development at Otis Elevator Company, believes should be asked—and aren't—are: "What do you need?" and "If you need it, do you want it?"

It seems to me that we continually lose sight of the truth: Adults need to see reasons for and values to them in learning. When they assess themselves, their strengths, their improvement and growth needs, they don't need anyone else to sell them on the value of the training, as long as it addresses their needs. Of course, I suspect the key word in the preceding sentence is "adults." In much of our training, I doubt whether the trainees feel as if they are being treated like adults. They've come to the training, Dick Hawkins says, "with a gun to their heads." To a very large extent, people are experts on themselves.

*It's an issue of ownership. There's a strong reluctance of HRD people to give up control to the line.*

Paul H. Chaddock
Senior Vice-President
Personnel
Lechmere, Inc.

Paul Chaddock has always insisted that "the direction for development is mutual." Both the HRD group and functional managers assume responsibility. In his operation, personnel and training specialists are "client centered" but not "client managed."

There is indeed an issue of ownership on both sides of the fence, as Paul Chaddock's comments suggest. If the training department holds the title, the design and delivery of programs will reflect the values of the HRD professionals, which may be fine generically or may be suitable for other companies but not their own. If management is sole owner, then management's values prevail, which could mean training when there is time, or training that is nice to have, or training that is based on fads to which management has become attracted. In such a climate, trainers may say, to use the words of Robert S. Fenn, who, in 1989, was national director of training at Travelers Insurance Companies: "We don't question it; we deliver it."

Scott Parry believes that many, trainers and managers alike, look at whatever training is delivered and say, "Well, it can't hurt. Maybe it could help." But it can hurt, for a very long time. Training that the trainees perceive as irrelevant, fanciful, a waste of time, otherworldly will often create a cynicism about the value of training that will in turn result in resistance to any further programs. You cannot have been in the training field for very long without having observed this phenomenon over and over. Gresham's law again: Bad training drives out good.

*Some training simply makes people feel good.*

Marianne Matheis
Head
Training and Development
The Aerospace Corporation

It's entertainment, Marianne Matheis says. Sue Thompson of Levi Strauss agrees: "A lot of management development is just charm school." Other trainers have used similar terms, such as "finishing school."

The people who feel good about such training are the trainees, the HRD people who receive happy evaluations immediately following the courses, and managers, who reassure themselves that their companies are doing something, and it's always nice when people enjoy that something. Unfortunately, as Richard Kropp points out, such training fails to demonstrate what he calls "value-addedness." Participants should emerge from the program potentially more effective than when they went in. The true evaluations are not on what trainers call smile sheets—the evaluations immediately after the course—but in the follow-up that occurs a month or two later that seeks to determine what the trainees are using on the job.

Training that isn't tied to improved performance can indeed be "expensive entertainment," as OD consultant Dianne H. Heard complains.

*Management training is often disconnected from strategic thinking and job reality.*

Badi G. Foster
President
Aetna Institute
for Corporate Education
Aetna Life and Casualty Company

This is probably the biggest single issue. Badi Foster believes that in traditional management training there has been far more emphasis on the acquisition of skills than on their application. In line with that thinking, Mal Warren of CVS advocates "less mediacy and more immediacy." His play on words is striking: There should be less concern with the conveying of new knowledge and more with the immediate application of the skills. Jim McMillin, vice-president of HRD at Bull Worldwide Information Systems, who agrees that training can be disconnected from the needs of the organization, believes also that there should be "a shift from knowledge critical to skills critical."

This particular issue, connecting training with the strategic thinking, the culture, the job reality, drives this book. For both trainers and managers, I preach decreasing the importance of the classroom and increasing the importance of the development that takes place on the work scene. I quite agree with Al Versacci of Amerada Hess who feels that there is just so much that formalized education can do. Most development, he maintains, takes place in the boss-subordinate relationship. Even there, or perhaps especially there, the trainer's role is valuable. Trainers and managers need each other to develop effectiveness in other managers and supervisors. John W. Dreyer, vice-president, executive resources and organization at Wakefern Food Corporation, says he doesn't even believe in most training. He does believe in orientation and perhaps certain basic skills training. But the rest, he believes, "should directly support what you're trying to accomplish or change in the organization."

*There's no appreciation for critical mass.*

Karin Kolodziejski
Manager
Field Training
Tektronix Inc.

For significant change in an organization, enough people have to be trained in the requisite skills and cultural values. Robert Fenn of Travelers echoes this need. There are often, he says, "too few to effect change." There is no more forceful argument for linking training and development to strategic thinking. Training programs that come and go, that are based on fads, that are intermittent and not continuing, that are generic rather than focused on real needs in the people and the organization are not going to produce critical mass. And critical mass is absolutely essential to change and improvement.

## Looking Ahead to a New Reality

I should add that the many experienced trainers I interviewed don't follow the traditional practices they criticize. But I suspect we've all been exposed to them, maybe in some cases even guilty of practicing them in years gone by. The importance of my interviews is to reinforce my thesis that so many of our training and development approaches in the past, indeed, for several decades, have not been effective, or at least not as effective as we needed them to be.

But there's another glaring truth about the interviews. Common threads run through their comments: Management training must reflect the needs of the organization and of the individuals trained. What goes on in the classroom must match the realities of the workplace. What has been taught in the classroom must be applied on the job. What is applied on the job must be reinforced by the trainees' managers. Training and development are a continuing process. Both management and HRD people have to work together to create training and development that are realistic and effective, that actually produce managers who can manage people and get the desired results from them.

Greater involvement is the key, for both trainers and managers. Trainers must be more committed to helping to run the business, and managers must be more purposeful in codesigning training that meets their needs. Both must also better understand the adult developmental process. Otherwise we continue to waste so many of our training dollars.

# PART TWO

# A Six-Step Program
# for Trainers and Managers

In recent years, while shaping ideas that were to go into books and articles, I've often tested them during presentations and speeches, usually at ASTD functions. For example, power issues were the subject of my presentation at the Atlanta conference of national ASTD in 1987. Subsequently I wrote *Power, Influence, and Your Effectiveness in Human Resources* (1988b). In 1989, I continued my periodic assessment of my recommendations for motivation training for managers, and those recommendations are a theme of Part Two. The following six steps formed the core of my presentation to about 300 participants at the Orlando, Florida, ASTD conference in May 1990.

The evaluations received at this presentation reinforced my belief that I was on to a real issue, and you're now reading about it. But one of the negative comments surprised me at first: "Nothing much new here." This feedback didn't seem to reflect the majority view but still, mulling it over, I realized that I identified with the judgment. What I was saying was new and it was not new. It was conventional wisdom and it was unconventional wisdom. Yes, I'm describing a paradox, something that I've grown more comfortable with in past years.

Probably what I said in Orlando was not really new to some of the training professionals in the audience. After all, I built my presentation on sound and familiar psychological realities: People are goal-driven; people need to have good reasons to learn in order to commit themselves to learning; for true learning, there must be application; desired behavior, such as new learned behavior, should be reinforced or rewarded; there should be collaborative relationships between trainers and their clients. The presentation didn't offer a blinding glimpse of the obvious perhaps, but there were many things said that trainers had heard before.

There's another sense, however, in which the ideas in Part Two are not necessarily new to trainers. Many of them have heard each of the recommendations. But what may be fresh for them, what may justify their attention, is that I'm strongly advocating that all six steps are necessary. We need to operate as a system. They are not just desirable practices—they are essential—all of them. I'm reasonably sure that most experienced HRD professionals have looked at these practices and said, "Someday, we'll be able to do them." That someday is now.

Finally, continuing the paradox, there's a vast difference between newness of concept or idea and newness of practice. You can look at a concept that has been around for a time and deny its newness, but the practice or application may justify the label of newness. The perspective in which trainers view the idea makes all the difference. Years ago, I read a newly published book by two men active in the burgeoning organization development movement. I agreed with the theories and concepts, but I didn't find anything startling or unfamiliar about the bases on which the authors built their book. A friend of mine, however, a highly respected manager of training and OD in his company, commented admiringly on the book. I told him that his favorable remarks surprised me, because I hadn't seen anything special. "That's because you're not a practitioner," he said. I deserved the rebuke, which is what it was. I had been looking at the book as a reviewer might; he had read it looking for ways to *apply* the concepts, and he had found them.

In addition, although trainers may be familiar with these concepts, this doesn't mean that managers are as knowledgeable in these areas, which is why, incidentally, this book is being written with functional managers in mind as the primary audience. Many managers are not up on their grasp of psychological principles. We might be rather deficient human resource people if we were not, but many managers can attest to many years of success in fulfilling their responsibilities without Psychology 101. The world is changing, however, causing me to recall some predictions I made around 1970 to the effect that eventually all managers would need to understand the psychology of people at work. That's one of the few predictions I ever made that I still subscribe to. For managers as well as trainers, then, my ideas may constitute some points that bear some hard analyzing. Managers too will need to know how to apply them.

So if you're a trainer or a manager considering these six steps as a system for the first time, and if you're searching for ways to apply them, you'll probably judge this book as having something new to say to you. But newness isn't the important factor. As we salespeople say, newness is a feature. The practicality is the benefit. Each of the six steps, listed below, enjoys its own chapter in Part Two.

1.  Forming collaborative relationships
2.  Establishing learning contracts
3.  Delivering training that motivates
4.  Using line managers as trainers
5.  Providing experiential learning and reinforcement
6.  Aligning reward systems with training goals

# ■ 3 ■

# Forming
# Collaborative Relationships

In many organizations, the relationship between the training department (staff) and the functional line management is tenuous or ill defined at best. To begin with, trainers can be quite contradictory in their perceptions of themselves and their departments. On the one hand, they might see themselves as isolated, and on the other, they may act in such a way as to reinforce that isolation. To elaborate, they are traditionally staff and usually considered to be a cost center, easily expendable in hard times. As such, they feel vulnerable and relatively powerless. I've confirmed the perception of powerlessness through the years by stating it as a fact before groups of trainers and watching the nodding heads throughout the room. And the sense of vulnerability is easily evident when you study the mobility of trainers. Being phased out or downsized is almost an everyday phenomenon.

However, if you take a poll among trainers as to what business publications they read on a regular basis, you will find that many have not developed the practice of reading what their clients find necessary: the *Wall Street Journal, Fortune, Business Week,* and others. An astonishingly large group of trainers, largely coming out of the education field, know little about business and the private sector; they can't speak the language of their clients; and when they use the jargon of human resources, the gap widens between them and those clients.

Collaborative relationships imply equality. It's not that the parties are all the same, but it is true that in a collaborative relationship between a trainer and a functional manager, there must be mutual understanding and respect. The trainer wants the client to regard him or her as a credible authority in training and development. The client/manager expects the trainer to regard him or her as an expert in the operation. As a psychologist might say, each of the parties often has his or her wants and expectations frustrated or violated.

There is also admittedly a power issue. As a group, people in human resources have been slow to recognize the kinds of power that are available to them. As a group, managers tend to be more aware of the sources of power and how they can be drawn on. Thus, there are power gaps, credibility gaps, and communication gaps, which have prevented many trainers and managers from establishing constructive working relationships with each other.

I don't think that many of us are realistic about training. The trainer in a friendly environment may say, "My company is very supportive of training." And the manager in the same company may say, "I have a lot of money in my budget for training." And both may miss the point widely. It isn't the verbal or financial support, necessarily. It's much more how people in the organization see training. If training is seen as an adjunct or an ancillary activity, no matter how esteemed it is, the perspective is faulty.

The reality is that training is essential to the success of all of us, individually and collectively. We must grow. We must advance in our skills, competence, and knowledge. There's no such thing as standing still. There's no such thing as maintenance of the existing state. Entropy will take care of that. There is an automatic decline in bodies that do not grow.

To say, therefore, that "we support training" is somewhat equivalent to saying that it is good to give to the arts, or to health care, or to community action. It's nice to do. It may result in a better quality of life. But we're not talking these days about a mere better quality of life, although we very much want to enjoy that. We may be talking about survival. In fact, we are talking about survival.

Training, for most of us and our companies, can mean the difference between decline and prosperity. And in a fiercely competitive world, decline leads to extinction.

The trainer says, "My function is to train." The manager says, "My function is to manage." What's the connection? Years ago, when I was a young man starting out in the business of writing and advising about management, a wise man said to me, "Managing is a function of training." Up to that time, I had believed the reverse: Training is a function of managing. Actually both premises are true, but one is vastly more important than the other: Managing is a function of training. The primary responsibility of a manager is to maintain an effective work group. (Strictly speaking, that's a contradiction in terms. Maintenance management is regressive. Entropy again.) But the environment in which the managing is done is constantly changing. There are always new threats, new challenges, new opportunities, new people, new politics, new market forces, and all constitute a need to adjust, adapt, stay flexible, and be responsive. There is a pronounced need for new skills, increased competence, deeper and broader knowledge, and training can provide all of that.

## Different Worlds

Through many of the years in which I have been in the training field and active in ASTD, trainers have often complained about their status and influence (more to the point, their lack of it) in their organizations. Traditionally, HRD people—in fact, all human resource professionals—have tended to perceive themselves as relatively powerless. That perception has been reinforced within and outside the field. I remember being appalled when I heard a management consultant who specialized in corporate change tell a group of trainers that they could play a valued role in change in their organizations if only they had influence, which, he added, they did not.

Line managers sometimes reinforce the trainers' perception of being uninfluential. "Me line, you staff," their words and behaviors say. In short, the line managers assert that the power and usually the money exist on their side of the gulf. Trainers frequently see themselves as having to sell their ideas and programs to the functional managers.

I'll say unequivocally that when trainers and managers see themselves in different worlds, with high fences between them, quality of training suffers, and because the training suffers, the total performance of the organization also suffers. After thirty years in this business, I cannot any longer believe that we can ensure the delivery of quality training and effective managers without close collaboration between HR people and their clients, the functional managers. Not cooperation, but collaboration. The former may be forced, but the latter is voluntary. Collaborators see mutual gains in working together. If your organization does not foster and reinforce collaboration in your supervisory and management training, you risk losing much of your investment, and you will be left with uncertain performance from your subordinates.

### Training Traditions

Few people have been more critical of the training profession and its members than I. The bottom line of my concern is that trainers themselves have done the most to perpetuate the image of training as a wimpy profession. Trainers often laugh when I apply the word "wimpy" to others' perceptions of us, but they also know that it is true.

Let's look at some of the reasons why our clients so often fail to see us as worthy partners. In the last two decades, the training field has grown enormously. In the final years of the 1970s, the New York Metro chapter of ASTD doubled its membership. Who were these entrants to the field? Many of them came from the education field, but very few came out of the university with the aim of being trainers. At that time, most people who found their way into the field had not, until recently, contemplated the idea of making training their career. To a large extent, the previous sentences describe today's scene, with the exception that colleges and universities offer formal education for people who want to enter the human resource and organization development fields. Many of these educators found training an attractive alternative because they believed that their skills in academic life were portable. They knew how to develop curricula and programs and to teach students. Some of them had excellent presentation skills—for the classroom. Their belief, however, was somewhat simplistic.

What follow are my general impressions of many of the people who have entered the field with the above perceptions. I distrust generalizations; in fact, I'm fond of saying that all generalizations are false, including this one. There have been many exceptions to what I'm about to describe.

Many who constituted this rapid influx had little theoretical background. For example, they knew little of the work that I referred to in my preface. They didn't know organizational behavior. Probably the only conceptual foundation they had was what they learned in train-the-trainer or certification programs. (If you are to use certain copyrighted courses, you must be certified by the holders of that copyright.) Their knowledge of the field and the research that is so helpful to us was quite limited.

Coming from the public sector, few understood corporate life, a fact that initially made it difficult for them to get jobs. Once inside, their effectiveness was severely limited by their inability to understand the needs and language of the people they had to deal with. Some adapted very quickly, however, but others remained comparatively isolated. Functional managers and executives often looked upon these ex-educators as anything but movers and shakers, were scornful of their importance, and were skeptical of their value to the company. And those trainers who didn't get involved with helping to run the business broadcast, perhaps unwittingly, an arrogance which further constrained them. It is hardly tactful to suggest to a client, through your behavior, that you don't regard his or her concerns as worthy of your study.

## Powerlessness

In part because they had experienced powerlessness in the public sector, trainers accepted it in the private sector as well. That acceptance has been unfortunate, if only because it often discouraged trainers from seeking equality and partnership with their clients. Too many trainers have continued to exist in a rarefied atmosphere. They see themselves as running training departments and programs rather than as key players in helping to run the corporation, a self-image that hardly earns them points with line managers. They develop programs and then try to persuade their organizational clients to subscribe to them. In fact, any time you run a short course in how to sell your ideas and programs to management, you can expect a pretty good-sized audience of trainers. Some training departments have created some impressive catalogues of courses available to their clients.

Lacking influence and prestige, other trainers have found themselves at the beck and call of their clients, who have their own ideas of what kind of training should be offered. Much of it is inappropriate and ineffective, but you'll find some trainers are grateful to be called on at all. They will offer the training, even though they suspect it may not help much. I have often criticized some of my colleagues for their seemingly uncritical acceptance of the fad of the moment. For one thing, the fad is easy to sell, if it is well known. And I have warned other trainers of what I regard as excessive reliance on outside trainers. If the training department becomes known as primarily a booking agency for external experts, why should top management be terribly sorry to ax the department when the budgets are cut? They don't see the training department as an irreplaceable resource.

Trainers' teaching background often influences their design of training. They create curricula much as they would in school, curricula that may not address the priorities of their clients and trainees. What seems logical may not in fact be. One of the important theses of this book is that it may *seem* proper to teach motivation as a subset of leadership or interpersonal skills, but considering the demands of the managerial responsibility, the emphasis should be on the reverse. Motivation is the most important management function and should enjoy primacy in training.

Their value of presentation skills may lead them into regarding the methodology of delivery as more important than anything else, even content. In fact, for years the most common complaint we heard uttered against trainers was that form preceded content, content did not shape the form. What is to be delivered is not as important as how it is delivered. Consequently, trainers as an audience will not surprisingly give high marks to the use of visuals and handouts and technology even when the content of the presentation is thin. Conversely, I have witnessed much grumbling among trainers when the delivery was unsophisticated but the content was very much the opposite.

Even though I believe we are still a long way from establishing professional standards in the HRD field, we have many people who are forging the way toward more power for trainers. We have our bright, skilled, articulate people in the field. A good representative is Karen Stein-Townsend, with whom I had an enjoyable interview that has been reproduced in Part Three. Karen's staff in the professional development division of Johnson & Higgins are all into the insurance business. They may all be trainers and consultants, but they see themselves as helping J&H to be even more successful in its business.

### The Quality of Involvement

Recognizing the need for HRD people to be involved in running the operation is probably what distinguishes the most professional trainers from the portraits that I've painted in the preceding paragraphs. Involvement means that they must be effective and valued resources. They must be good at training and understanding the business, the mission, the concerns of their clients.

I've repeatedly cited one excellent example of involvement. She joined the training department of a very large bank. In her ten years there, she learned about banking, serving as assistant branch manager at one point. Taking advantage of the opportunities offered by the bank, she earned her M.B.A. in finance and became certified as a financial planner. Subsequently she went to work for a Wall Street firm and took the Series 7, the exams that qualify one for a broker's license. Again, seizing the opportunities, she earned another master's degree, her third, taking mostly computer courses. I'm not suggesting that every trainer ought to earn three master's degrees, but her involvement in each of the businesses she has been in is exemplary.

### Management and Training

If I've been known to be tough on my training colleagues, I can be quite acerbic toward my managerial colleagues. From time to time

I take them to the woodshed for their lack of seriousness about training for their supervisors and managers. First of all, too few of them seem to insist on quality in their training. I suspect that many of them feel that it is an obligatory thing, that you really must be prepared to provide it and pay for it without expecting significant results. And that is utter nonsense. You can get the results you want and are probably not getting if you become sufficiently involved in the process, which is what this book is all about.

There are some of you out there who don't really want management training to work very well. It's threatening. When people return to the workplace with sound new methods of managing that are contrary to the way you manage, you stifle their practice. You find ways of discouraging the newly returned managers from practicing the principles they've been exposed to. Or you abdicate your responsibilities in the process and expect the supervisors and managers to try to apply the new learning with no backup or help from you. Your obligation, it would seem to me, is to make sure your investment pays off, although when it doesn't, you freely blame the training department and/or the trainees.

Some of you dictate to the training department. "I want this," you say, and you don't tolerate much difference of opinion. After all, you're paying for it, aren't you? You're the line manager; you know best. That entitles you to set the rules of the game. You can really get into the fads, too. A respected colleague of mine in training recalls being at a meeting of top managers and listening to one companion rave about a new program that most of us in the field believed was sheer malarkey. But she told me, "I knew I didn't dare say a word against the program. He was convinced it was the last word."

And please, let's stop all this traditional management talk about how management training is "soft stuff." It has all the value and feasibility to you of nailing gelatin to the wall. Granted, some of the trainers you deal with may share your outmoded opinion, but you should know better. For many years, we have known what we need to know about how people work best. There's nothing tentative about it: We know what works; we know how to train your managers in what works; it's hard stuff. I have very mixed feelings when someone applies what I've taught or written and tells me in amazement, "It really worked!" Of course, it did. I'm glad for the reinforcement, but I'm a bit annoyed that the trainee was surprised.

One other thing very much annoys me. Too many of you are constantly looking for miracles, placebos, and panaceas as the short route to total change and success. You like simplistic approaches because you mistake simplistic for simple. Simple is best, and simplistic is impossible. You therefore directly or through your training department engage consultants and trainers like me to come give your people a crash course in something or other. For example, you say to me, "Come in and do a day on motivation." In my world, motivation is the very essence of managing, and you want me to cover it in seven or eight hours. I can do it, I love to take your money, but warn you that there won't be much learning. That is simply too much knowledge to impart in too little time. You will probably respond to me, "This is all I have budgeted."

Or you call me up and say, "Our management group has a rough time making decisions. There's a lot of backbiting and suspicion and competition. Can you help us operate more effectively in our problem solving?" Sure I can. I spend a day with you and your folks, and I usually find a way to unblock you; your group actually makes a decision, and you say, "Thanks a lot." I caution you, however, that one day and one good experience are not going to turn your group around. Old behaviors will reassert themselves. You shrug and reply, "Yes, we should probably do some follow-up, but there's no time."

Here is the heart of what I must tell you:

- You must not expect someone from outside your department to have total control over that development. You must be involved.
- You have every right—and an obligation—to insist that your investment in training produce a reasonable result. The training must be worthwhile for your subordinates and for you.
- The continuing development of your subordinate supervisors and managers will take place only if you help them develop their skills. They depend on you for that, and you know them and your needs better than anyone else. Otherwise, chances are you've thrown away a lot of your training dollars.

Finally, please accept my assurance that your people, or the vast majority of them, want to improve, to grow, to become more effective. Offer training and development with the recognition that they want it as much as you, that they recognize the need for it even more than you. Always introduce the idea of training to your people as "Here's the opportunity for you," not "Here's a way to fix your shortcomings."

### Achieving Partnership

For the sake of more effective management training, avoid the twin evils: training-by-catalogue and client-dominated training. The training department may offer standardized programs (recall Scott Parry's description: One size fits all). When selling the program or course to you, the trainer may tell you which other managers or departments have already gone through the program. He or she may show you favorable evaluations. These are fine backups, but the most important consideration for you is whether the program being discussed will meet your very specific needs. The first appropriate question is, "What benefits are in this program for us?" Talk about results and outputs. Trainers can be very fond of inputs. I heard a trainer boast that her department had put more than 600 people through a time-management program. She belongs to the AOC school of training: asses on chairs. The important questions are "What happened as a result of all that training?" "Were the trainees able to increase productivity by 22 percent?" "How was that measured?"

Other appropriate questions are "Who will deliver or conduct the training?" "What are this person's credentials?" The fact that he or she may have given the program several times to others is secondary to whether his or her background lends itself to your needs. As a consultant and trainer, I've sometimes been asked whether I do a particular kind of work. When I answer yes, the next question is "Who have been some of your clients?" That's ridiculous. They should worry more about how I do it or how capable I am. I might add that consultants and free-lance trainers who routinely list their clients for me make little impression. I know that what I have done for ABC Corporation may have little relevance in that form for the XYZ organization. The fact that I can talk knowl-

edgeably about motivation in retail sales personnel does not prom-
ise that I can be equally competent in addressing the concerns of
nuclear chemists.

Another question might be whether the course could or
should be customized for your people. Granted, there are some programs that are useful even though they are generic, for example,
presentation or writing skills. Some overview courses, such as principles of managing for new managers, might be acceptable. But
you'll want to satisfy yourself that the design and delivery of the
course are targeted for your audience. After all, you're going to have
to oversee the application and the further development of your
trainees.

There are a number of important inputs that perhaps only
you can provide. What will your staffing requirements be for the
year or two ahead? Will you expand or contract? Will your group
be taking on additional responsibilities or turning out new products or services? Will your department be reorganizing, say, into
project teams or self-managed work groups? Such factors could
create the need for different kinds of skills. This is information that
your training department must have to give you what you want and
need. You may have to translate the information you have about
your needs for them, show them how what you need can be worked
into the training.

You are looking for a dialogue, a negotiation. "Here's what
I need," you say. "How can you help me?"

*Assessing Needs.* The trainer will probably want to spend time with
you and with your people to make his or her own assessment of your
training needs. One benefit that may emerge from this preliminary
study is that training is not what you really need. For example, you
may have some interpersonal conflicts that point to the necessity for
behavior changes in the disputants rather than a course in how to
manage conflict. We've come a long way from believing that training can fix whatever is wrong, or "If you don't know what to do,
train somebody." Too many dollars have disappeared down that
hole.

Some organizations have insisted that their trainers take on
consulting roles with clients, or a consulting intervention, or team

building to help those managers understand better what they and their departments need in the way of training. I thoroughly believe in this, because in my definition consultants do not sell products. They should not be pushing a catalogue or off-the-shelf item.

Those of us who have sold to businesspeople have become accustomed to the cliché "my business is different." If the objection is used to avoid listening to the salesperson or having to think about what he or she is saying, it's obstructive. But there is, as in all clichés, a basic truth: Of course your business is different, in terms of your style of managing, mix of people, mission, methods of operating, and so on. The consultant/trainer must acknowledge this reality.

*Matching Expectations.* Don't contract for any program until you are reasonably sure that what the training department expects to be able to deliver to you matches your expectations. The design and delivery are important, of course, and there should be a firm agreement on what will go into them. But more important are the mutual expectations of outcome. What does the trainer believe will happen as a result of the training? What do you expect and want as a result of the course?

You must be totally explicit about the expected outcomes. Don't assume that you and the trainer understand each other's expectations. As a trainer and consultant, I can testify that whatever disappointments I've experienced were largely due to the different expectations the client and I had. Usually I felt the client was unrealistic, that is, expected much more than I knew I could deliver under the conditions. But I have to blame myself for not having gone the extra length to ensure that both of us had the same outlook.

Pin the trainer down. Accept the possibility that he or she cannot give you everything you want, considering constraints of time and money and the people involved, but you should know of any limitations in advance. And the trainer should be well aware that you may want more than he or she expected to have to deliver. In short, you must be prepared to pare down your expectations; the trainer should be ready to raise his or hers.

*Forms of Partnership.* Obviously when you sit down with a representative of the training department jointly to prepare a course or a program, and when the two of you meet as respected equals, you've formed a partnership. At its core you bring your needs and knowledge of your people and the operation; the trainer brings a problem-solving background with a wide knowledge of the solutions that can be developed for you. Ideally.

Some training directors like to have a committee in the unit to be trained to help design and to oversee the program. On the committee would be the trainers involved, functional managers, and perhaps even some of the trainees. Some training directors tell me that they won't do work in a department or a division unless such a committee is formed.

Some organizations maintain training advisory boards on which can be found trainers, functional managers, high-level executives, and other staff people. These boards, which change membership perhaps every year, review the mission and strategy of the organization and assess training needs. This kind of partnership, which is top down, can be very effective in determining the needs of the organization and maintaining the quality of the training.

In your department, you may act as liaison in management training and development, or delegate the authority and responsibility to a subordinate. The essential thing is that in any management training program you are represented along with the training department. Training must be a joint concern. After all, they're your people, and it's your money. You have a right to get what you need.

### For Trainers

While the primary audience for this book is the functional manager, I feel the need to append a segment here for trainers; I urge them to think partnership as well. For several years, I've been telling HRD people that they are probably not drawing on the available sources of power and using the influencing skills that are easily acquired.

I advocate that you learn basic selling skills (everyone should have them), not because you need to sell your programs so much as to learn how to think in terms of the client's needs, or at least how the client perceives those needs. Then you must use the appropriate language to demonstrate that your expertise can meet those needs. And the language you use, of course, is the client's. I shudder when I hear training people use our jargon—the psycho-babble of OD specialists. That sort of talk can turn clients off very quickly. In Chapter Ten, I talk at length about selling skills, since I believe firmly that they should be part of management training. You may also find them interesting and useful from a personal standpoint.

There is no reason why HR people should feel a lack of power, as I argue in my book *Power, Influence, and Your Effectiveness in Human Resources* (1988b). I identify twelve sources or kinds of power, many of which are available to you. You should regularly add to and strengthen your power base—a very legitimate activity for anyone in organizational life. Let me extract some of the more obvious power sources.

*Competence power.* This means that the more you know the training field and your organization's operation, the more power you can accumulate. You cannot, in my opinion, be influential without having competence power. If you are not perceived as knowing what you are doing, if you are not viewed as a helpful resource, you cannot expect to be credible. I often ask training audiences about the extent of their reading of both training literature and business publications, and I'm very disappointed to see the relatively low readership in either category.

*Personal power.* You've seen this in some of your clients—the way they walk, talk, and carry themselves, the confidence they project, the ease with which they relate to others. Much of that power comes from their knowing that they are competent. The awareness of competence builds self-confidence, another component of personal power.

*Resources power.* You have resources power when you have something that others need and cannot easily obtain from another source. One trainer told me about a call he received from a division manager: "I want you to get me someone who can talk to us about MBO." The trainer replied: "I don't have to get you someone. When do you want me?" Understand your organization as best you can, what the needs of the clients might be. Then broadcast that you are capable of filling those needs.

*Alliance power.* How many ways can you find to ally your-self with the managers you deal with? By yourself you may be able to do little, but when you are perceived as having the support of many people in your organization, you have alliance power. You have influence proportionate to the number of people who are willing to talk for you, to enlist support for you, to work for you in your training. Closely related is reward power: You can reward outstanding results of training and the consequent excellent performance by publicizing it, by seeing that the managers responsible for it get recognition throughout the organization. That's a good way to build alliances.

*Professional power.* You can build power within the organization by what you do outside. Publish; make presentations to professional groups; be a volunteer in professional associations. Soon people who work with you will recognize that your professional colleagues esteem you and will be persuaded that you deserve their esteem as well.

There is no reason for any trainer to continue to feel powerless and without influence in the organization. There are simply too many ways you can build your power base. Why shouldn't you? Your clients do, and they'll respect, trust, and believe you more if you come to the table with them as a powerful equal.

# ■ 4 ■

# Establishing
# Learning Contracts

At present, trainers generally seek contracts with the people whom they are to train, and they look for contracts with their clients. But the third side of this triangle is not so common. There is a need for managers to sit down with their subordinates before the training to discuss some important terms. For example, what should the training cover? What should the benefits be for the trainee, the manager, and the department/organization? How will the learning be applied on the job? Also, there should be a clear understanding that the trainee is to take responsibility for his or her learning.

In more than twenty years with one corporation, I cannot remember when my boss and I sat down to discuss what was going to or should happen as a result of the training. I doubt whether my experience was unique. Managers are busy, often putting out fires, or they assume that the surbordinate knows what should happen, or they expect the trainer to be in charge of the process. Bad business, all of it. All of us need goals. If trainees aren't clear about what is important in the training process, or what they are expected to practice back on the job, or what the boss will reward them for, training can be a pretty murky business. Too often, it is also eminently forgettable.

Why don't trainers insist on these learning contracts? Without organizational support, especially from the top, they may be hesitant to go into the client's operation and make sure the contracting process takes place. That is the kindest reason I can offer. If I were to be unkind, I might even suggest that some trainers don't realize just how vital these pretraining interviews between boss and subordinate are.

Too many managers probably don't understand how much it is in their interest to maintain control over the training. I've written elsewhere that training is too important to be left to trainers. The trainers, no matter how familiar they are with the operation, will never know as well as the manager his or her needs and the resources he or she must work with.

## Types of Contracts

In any training situation, there should be at least three contracts. The first is between the trainer and the manager who is responsible for the training. The second is between the trainer and the learners. And the third ties the learner to his or her manager. The first two sometimes take shape. The third is, I sense, fairly rare. The first, between the manager and the trainer, I discussed in Chapter Three. There really is no excuse for the trainer and the manager to overlook the contract. There are some trainers who slide by the need for a firm and explicit contract with their trainees. And probably few managers understand just how important it is for them to have a contract with each subordinate who is about to enter training.

Just as it is essential for the manager to assume responsibility for the training and the development of his or her subordinates, it is vitally important that the trainee take responsibility and become accountable for the training. The training is an investment for you, the manager. You pay for it, directly or indirectly. Even if there is no monetary outlay from your budget, you still have indirect costs in the time in which the subordinate is away from the job, and there may be travel costs as well. You should protect your investment.

Basically, the contract between you and the learner consists of your agreeing about what will happen as a result of the training. There should be a thorough discussion of why the training is taking place. What are the department's needs? What are the trainee's needs? Compare your expectations of what will take place with those of the trainee.

For example, the training session will deal with appraisal techniques. What is the goal of the training? What will happen as a result of it? The subordinate will be better equipped to evaluate the value of employees' performance to the department and the organization as a whole. What does "better equipped" mean? It could mean that the judgments that the manager makes are in the perspective of higher goal achievement. Through the appraisals, the management trainee will be able to help employees develop action plans as well as skills to achieve higher goals than before. The manager will also be able to assess employees' needs for further development. The appraisals will show closer agreement between how the manager sees an employee's performance and how the employee sees his or her performance.

The outputs can be measured in the closeness of the agreements, as mentioned above; the plans and schedules for employee training and development; the joining in the goals that fulfill the needs of the department; and, after the first appraisal period, the achievement of the goals that had been established during the previous appraisal. In short, was the performance improved through better appraisal techniques?

The inputs are important—the planning, the interviewing, the goal-setting, the agreements, the relative harmony. But the inputs can only really be judged successful if the outputs are what they should be—the total performance, the total upgrading of the effectiveness of individuals and the department.

### How Adults Learn

Not to take time to establish a learning contract is to gamble. As manager, you can only hope that the trainee understands why this is important to him or to her and to the department. If you don't know what you're supposed to achieve, you can't know when you've been successful. And many trainees don't know. They put in the time, sit through the sessions, listen to the trainer, then come back and experiment with some new behavior. If it isn't what the manager expected when he or she authorized the training, the trainee will get the message: Don't do that again. Chances are, what will happen in many cases is that there won't be any further experimentation of any sort, and no learning. (It reminds one of Mark Twain's comments about the cat who sits on a hot stove. The cat won't do it again—but the cat won't sit on a cold stove either.)

We learn when we have a reason to learn, one that is valuable to us. Will it help us to feel more competent and sure of ourselves? Does it open up the opportunity for advancement? Will the boss like and respect us more? Will we get more satisfaction out of what we do? Will the job be more fun? Do we increase our chances of survival if we take on the training?

Once we have the content of the training, we need a chance to apply it or practice it. If we don't get that chance, not only are we frustrated but we probably won't retain the knowledge; most of it will have been forgotten in two or three months. The value of much management training simply evaporates.

While we are trying to practice and apply the learning, we need feedback from a credible source, which means either the manager or a mentor. Finally, when we have been successful in demonstrating the new behavior or skills, we need to be reinforced, rewarded. Sometimes the reward can be spelled out as part of the contract: "You'll be ready to step into the supervisor's position of the auditing section," or "You'll be heading up the new telemarketing group." Perhaps you can't be specific about more money or an advancement or more responsibility, but you can suggest internal rewards, those the subordinate generates for himself or herself. "You'll truly feel part of the professional group when you finish the course." "The work will be more satisfying to you because you'll be able to do a greater variety of tasks." "When you reach that level of competence, you'll have a right to feel very proud of your accomplishments." "You'll have a lot of new status around here, because you'll be the first to complete this kind of program."

One of the simplest, clearest, and most effective learning contracts I ever saw was connected with my first job. I was a trainee for a large life insurance company in the group benefits department. The entire training program was laid out for me: This is what you have to master, and this, and this; when you have done so, you'll have your own branch office and the chance to start making commissions on the business your office produces; the sooner you complete the training, the sooner you're out of here. It worked just fine. The average period of training, I was told, was one year. I was out in nine months.

*Training as a Reward.* Training can be a reward, or the employee may well see it that way. Frederick Herzberg has shown in his research that advancement and possibility for growth are motivators. Training can open the door to both. Furthermore, training can be evidence of improved performance and increased competence. "Your basic writing skills are fine, and I'd like to see you take on the advanced writing skills course."

You might offer a subordinate a chance to acquire skills that may not be immediately required in the job or for his or her growth today but will be useful eventually. I've talked often about how in the late 1970s my boss offered me the opportunity of going to the University of Virginia for a three-day course in public speaking skills. "They might come in handy someday." I saw her invitation as an acknowledgment of my value to the department and consequently as a reward.

You might be able to establish an obvious progression from basic and simpler skills training to more complex and advanced courses. Your subordinate can see that if he or she is successful at learning and applying new skills (probably the same thing) at the lower levels of sophistication, much more challenging learning lies ahead.

*Buying into Training.* You want to encourage the employee to buy into the training by showing the value of the learning. The contract with its agreement on what the subordinate is to master and what may happen as a result of the mastery is a definite selling point. Smart trainers know how to encourage the buy-in. Before the session begins, they ask the participants to list their learning objectives. My question usually is "What would you like to take away from here at the end of the course? What would you like to be able to do that you can't do now, or to do better than you do it now?"

The wish list, as I call it, is updated throughout the course, and we frequently check it to make sure that we're addressing the issues that the trainees think are important to them. The wish list is my contract with them, and it accomplishes several things. First, people get a sense that they're going to get some personal benefits out of the program. For example, one management trainee might say, "I need to know how to criticize a couple of people who resist it, who get very defensive when I suggest they need to correct something they do." That goes on the list, and before breaking up, we make sure we cover it.

Another benefit of the wish list is that it signals the learners to take responsibility for making sure that they get at least some of what they want. I have no qualms about saying to them, "If you don't tell me what you need, it's your fault if you walk away from here unsatisfied. Don't sit on your hands and then complain that we didn't cover your needs."

A third benefit of the list of objectives is that it warns me of misplaced or unrealistic expectations in the learner. Quite simply, if the course objective is to spend one day on one-to-one communicating techniques, I'm probably not going to be able to get into presentation skills, so it's better to break that news in advance and to help the trainee adjust his or her expectations before the day starts. Also, the wish list encourages a focusing. In some cases, trainees bring to the session a lot of anger and frustration derived from their experiences with the organization. It's helpful to focus their attention on what we can accomplish during the session, so that it will not be a prolonged gripe session.

*Adjusting the Learning.* You as manager can work with your subordinate to develop a wish list also. Your partnership with the training professionals enables you to say to the trainee, "Here's what will be available for you. How does that look to you?" "Is this what you want?" "How do you see this benefiting you?" "Which of these techniques or skills do you see as most applicable to you on the job after you return?"

It may well be that the trainee will be able to offer suggestions for widening the scope or altering the focus to make the course more valuable, information you may choose to pass on to the trainers. The interview may reveal things about the trainee that you and the trainers need to know. To illustrate: You're about to send him or her off to a course on feedback skills—criticizing, appraising, and so on—but you notice that the person has much difficulty in listening to what you're saying, which may reinforce what you knew before about this person. It might be a good idea to pass this information on to the professionals. You say to them, "Maybe you can spend a little extra time with him on his listening." Or they and you might conclude that your subordinate needs a listening seminar before advancing to the feedback skills.

Just as the trainer's list of objectives might indicate some resistance to the session in the trainees, your interview might bring such negative feelings to the surface. They may not be what you'd like to hear, but it's far better to uncover them before rather than after. In some instances the resistance may be rooted in cynicism: Previous training hasn't accomplished what it was trumpeted as doing. In other cases, the opposition may stem from the subordinate's view that he or she doesn't need it. And in still other situations, the subordinate may feel insecure at the thought of leaving his or her responsibility.

I'm rather sympathetic to much of the cynicism I've encountered. In training sessions it comes out in the very beginning, if it comes out at all. The trainee is saying, "Hey, I went through this last year with the Primus program, and it wasn't worth much. Why do you think you're different?" I may respond with something such as, "It's up to you and me to make sure it is different, that you take away from here what you want." It's a nonconfrontational approach that usually eases the pressure long enough to get things working. This, essentially, can be your approach as a manager to such resistance: "We've worked with the training department to come up with a program that looks as if it meets our needs. But now we need you to make sure that it does. Today, let's talk about how you can help us to complete the circle." Bring the trainee into the learning process.

### The Manager's Influence

*Expressing Your Values.* When the subordinate throws up a barrier to the training, ostensibly in the belief that he or she is quite effective now, thank you, I'm convinced that the worst thing you can do is to order the subordinate to take the training, or to threaten him or her if it isn't undertaken. There may be a number of ways to say it, but what often comes out is, "Hey, do you want to get on my list?" You may be dealing with hard-core resistance. Even if the subordinate succumbs to your pressure, there may not be much learning. I can remember times when I faced a disruptive trainee who had come under protest. Such a person is often out to prove there is no worth to the training, and he or she will try to fulfill the prophecy for the others as well.

It's very risky to try to force people to take training. If the session is short, say one or two days, I will often, as a trainer, write the person off. I'll concentrate instead on the others, who are more committed. Any effort to go toe to toe with the recalcitrant trainee will only take precious time away from the others. If the training session is long enough—a week or two cumulatively—the other trainees themselves may be able to deal with the disruptive influence. They'll get tired of the negativism and will express their disapproval. The rebel will probably react more to their criticism than to any arguments or inducements offered by the trainer and at that point either will try to blend in with the others or will leave the group.

A soft response is better than a hard, direct one. Try a combination of what we at Research Institute of America called the illumination technique and an expression of your values. In using the illumination technique, you feed back to the person his or her own comments in a slightly exaggerated form. It might go something like this: "So you feel that there would be nothing of value to you anywhere in this course?" Most likely the resister will back off from that absolute statement: "Well, I didn't say there wouldn't be anything for me. I just don't believe it's worth the time." You reply: "You're saying that there's no way I could make my investment in your training worthwhile?" Probably there will be another backdown. You've softened him or her up.

Now find a way to let the subordinate know that you favor the training. You might say, "I want to give you every chance to make a decision here that you're sure of or that you're comfortable with. Let me just review with you what's going to be covered." After that, you continue, "I think you can see that I've worked very closely with the training department to make sure that the program represents my standards. I want a course that will help all of my supervisors perform according to my standards. If you sincerely believe that you will be able to work up to my standards without the training, I certainly won't ask you to take training that wouldn't help you at all."

Is there a threat? Of course. You're saying, in effect, "Every supervisor who reports to me will be evaluated according to the standards presented in this course. That means you, too. And if you can't meet the standards, because you haven't taken the training, you'll have to suffer the consequences. It's your risk." You have a right to insist that anyone who works for you perform according to your standards, so long as they are reasonable. The threat is perfectly within legitimate boundaries.

*Providing Reassurance.* You have a different kind of problem with the person who feels insecure about leaving his or her department even for two or three days. For a number of years, back in the late 1960s and early 1970s, I attended a number of management seminars around the country, and I was flabbergasted to see at every break long lines of people at the pay phones, desperately trying to call their offices. With this kind of nervousness, you'll do well to provide some reassurance that things will go well in his or her absence. The implication is that you're not going to look for ways to punish the subordinate if something goes wrong (although you'll find it helpful to encourage the supervisor to delegate more responsibility and train people to act in his or her absence). More important is your expression of your values, what is important to you, and therefore on what basis the supervisor will be evaluated. If you want to help a person change behavior, you must provide a more valuable reward than the person believes he or she is getting right now.

The insecure manager believes that he or she is best rewarded at this time in maintaining a hands-on presence in the department. You suggest that although that is important in your value system, what is even more important is that the person undertake the learning that you recommend. You thereby substitute a higher-level reward. As for reassurance, you can of course solve the problem temporarily by suggesting that the supervisor's subordinates come to you with problems they can't solve while the boss is away. But in the longer term, your bigger problem is to communicate to the supervisor that he or she needs to do some developmental work on subordinates to equip them to act confidently in his or her absence.

Did I join those long lines at the telephone? I called a couple of times, only to find that everything was going smoothly. I admit I had mixed feelings about no one missing me.

*Giving Positive Messages.* Your message to subordinates on training should be clearly positive: You will benefit from this; you will derive satisfaction from this; I can give you better evaluations; this is a growth opportunity for you; if you have been consistent in recognizing learning, honoring it, rewarding it, promoting it, you'll find yourself getting much more benefit from it than if you simply offer it neutrally, as some managers do.

But some managers, far from promoting or selling it, actually undermine the value of training before it can do good. Following are some of the ways managers discount learning.

*Presenting it as a fix-it.* The manager sees the subordinate as not OK, in the terms of Transactional Analysis. The message the subordinate gets is, "Go fix yourself." The manager indicates that the subordinate is not delegating enough, or seems to resist imposing disciplinary measures on erring employees, or is having problems getting along with co-workers. The message the subordinate gets is, "Here's a course that can help you with your problem." If the employee feels embarrassed, humiliated, resentful, put down, it's highly unlikely that he or she is going to achieve much learning and behavioral change.

All of us can benefit from some type of training or other to give us more knowledge or more ability to function, and that training by its very nature can imply filling what is an absence or a lack, but it should be presented as a growth experience, as an improvement rather than a deficiency correction. If you convey a conviction that no one is ever as effective in every situation as he or she would like to be, your subordinates will generally happily accept your recommendations for learning. It's hard to believe that anyone could disagree with or be threatened by that statement. The vast majority of us seek on a continuing basis to be more capable, more complete.

*Making training a command performance.* Many times the trainer in me shuddered when I saw how people were notified of the training. "This is to inform you that you are to report to . . ." or "You will be expected to participate in . . ." And there are other ways managers let subordinates know that this training is obligatory and not negotiable. The word has come down from on high. When I do training for an organization, I often ask the manager in charge how he or she intends to spread the word. Unquestionably, the attitude that many trainees have toward the training, their receptivity, their enthusiasm, depends on whether their boss or higher management acknowledges their maturity and dignity.

A little selling can do wonders to create an openness for the training. Tell subordinates what is being covered and why. Show them how they will benefit from the learning. Inform them where they can go to ask questions or get more information. In my view it is wrong to issue commands. It is much more productive to say, in short, "I know you won't want to miss this opportunity. Here's why."

*Discounting the value of the training.* Through the years, I've heard countless statements from managers to their subordinates that virtually dismiss the training as having little or no value. Try some of these: "I know it's a busy time for you, but if you don't go, my boss is going to be on my neck." "Look, I realize that this may be a waste of time, but we have to keep management happy." "You know, these trainers come up with these programs because they have to justify their jobs." "I know that it's a lot of BS, but you gotta play the game. Take the time out, go, relax, take a break. It'll look good on the old record." And here's my all-time favorite: "You never know when you might pick up something."

Of course, I wouldn't be realistic if I didn't acknowledge at the same time that the attitudes that lie behind some of the above statements have justification. Management does mandate programs that the trainee can't see the value of. There are trainers who build catalogues of programs that may have little relevance because the trainers have not bothered to learn the operation. And some of the programs are so generic that the trainee doesn't make the link between the classroom and the workplace. These flaws can be corrected only if management sees itself as partners with the training professionals and assumes equal responsibility for making sure that the trainee's time and energy are well spent.

*Some Benefits of Listening.* Any contract requires a certain amount of trust, and the learning contract demands quite a bit of it. If you want the subordinates to open up with you about how they see the training, their need for it, their benefits from it, you must build some trust in the relationship between the two of you. If you're fortunate enough to have achieved that trust, here are some of the things you might discuss with employees before training.

- *Coaching.* How to guide a subordinate to a decision or solution without doing the work for him or her. The kinds of questions that will guide the employee without leading. How to ask them.
- *Counseling.* How to develop and use documentation that can persuade an employee that you have justification for counseling. How to develop documentation that can reduce the risk of legal action if the employee is demoted or terminated. How to help the employee create an action plan for performance improvement and how and when to monitor the employee's progress—or lack of it—after the initial counseling session. How to handle the employee's anger or anxiety. How to deal with the manager's own anger. How to terminate an employee who has not turned around the poor performance.
- *Delegation.* How to use delegation as a reward or as a continuing learning program. How to identify those tasks that should be delegated and the appropriate employees for them. How to monitor. How to stay in control of delegated work. What to do in the case of unexpected failure of an employee to complete the assignment successfully. How much initial latitude to give to an employee in delegating.
- *Interviewing skills.* How to keep interviews on track. How to control them without dominating. How to use nondirective question techniques to get information. How to encourage employees to give feedback. What to do when the manager gets

information that creates defensiveness. How to overcome that
defensiveness.

- *Performance appraisal.* How to reduce the appearance of being
  arbitary. How to persuade employees to accept managers' evaluations. How to get away from the feeling that managers
  "grade" their employees. What to do when the employee strongly disagrees with the manager's appraisal.

The above are some of the concerns that both the subordinate
and you share. They may be translated into learning objectives and
become part of your learning contract.

### Outside Seminars

When you send a subordinate off to an outside seminar—the AMA,
a university, or such—you may lose one of your bargaining chips:
that you and the training department have worked together on the
program. But you can still have a learning contract. Discuss the
scope of the program. Decide what is important to both of you. Get
agreement on the learning objectives. And entrust the subordinate
with the responsibility of making his or her needs known to the
seminar conductor. The overall process is the same. In addition,
you'll want the subordinate to evaluate the worth of the seminar
and the trainer in the perspective of your training and development
needs.
   Your pretraining interview and follow-up are even more important in the case of outside training because you are placing an
extra burden on the subordinate. He or she must be able to translate
the generic content of the public seminar into meaningful application in your culture. Many people who simply are not adaptable or
flexible need help doing this. Your coaching before and after will
probably be very helpful and will increase the value of the learning
experience.

### Ongoing Coaching

Most managers are familiar with problem-solving coaching: The
subordinate brings you a problem and you work with him or her

to find a solution. But there's another kind of coaching that is longer term—coaching for the subordinate's growth and development. I have no evidence that convinces me that many managers do this. They get busy. The frequent complaint is that many managers are too self-absorbed, worrying too much about their own careers. (I suspect that's more true than the "busy" reason.) And it's always been a problem that some managers dislike the idea of coaching someone right out from under them.

The point is that true development takes place when the manager orchestrates it for his or her subordinates. The manager works with the subordinate to help him or her create a plan for growth and then provides opportunities for the subordinate to fulfill the plan.

In *The Manager's Motivation Desk Book* (1985), I provide several recommendations or questions for the manager who realizes the importance of coaching at least the better performing subordinates in their career growth:

1.  *Anticipate the departmental work that lies ahead.* Granted, seeing far ahead has become a risky business, but look at the next year or two. What new functions will make their appearance? What new skills will be required? What can you advise your valuable subordinates to help them take advantage of the work that may be around the corner? You're in a position to know better than they.

2.  *Specify the principal work assignments the employee will undertake in the next six or twelve months.* Is he or she prepared? What needs to be done to bring the subordinate up to the required skills and knowledge level?

3.  *What future events will offer challenges and opportunities for the employee?* Again, you're in the best position to know what's going on, or will be going on. Look over possible organizational changes, staffing changes, budget changes, new facilities, and new projects or plans. What do these mean for your more valued subordinates?

4.  *What can you do to prepare the employee to do a better job or take on more or different responsibility?* That's what your coaching is all about. It should be periodic as the signs of

opportunity or need appear and as the subordinate acquires more competence.

The training you prescribe or make available should be done in the context of your long-term coaching.

# ■ 5 ■

# Delivering Training
# That Motivates

This is undoubtedly the most radical of the six steps. Despite the critic mentioned in the introduction to Part Two who left the Orlando session saying that there was nothing new, it is not a widespread practice. I advocate training managers in the context of motivation for several reasons. First, management is a system, which I suspect many managers will be surprised to hear. It is not often presented that way, but rather it may seem to be a series of disconnected functions. Second, a system provides a context in which you can fit the various skills, and that aids retention. The memory curve is our greatest enemy. Third, teaching management in the context of motivation ensures instant and obvious relevance, because motivation of subordinates is the very essence of managing. If motivation is the context, it would be nearly impossible for the trainee to say, "This is just classroom theory."

However, the motivation theory must be easily translatable into practice. The only motivation theory I know that can quickly and simply be turned into practice is Expectancy Theory (discussed in Chapter One), which is strangely neglected. I know that it is, because everywhere I go, I ask trainers whether they know the theory, and if they do, whether they use it. Most don't know it, and few of them use it as their theory base. Most of the senior trainers interviewed acknowledge that their teaching in the area of motivation is really generic or eclectic. It does not seem to be an important subject, and it is almost always treated as a subset of something else, such as leadership or interpersonal skills. As an astute colleague of mine once said, "If it's Tuesday morning, it must be motivation."

I want to say here that the neglect of this underlying and vital management priority is one of the most puzzling aspects of the field of management training and development. There are millions of managers out there trying to win the commitment and the efforts of tens of millions of subordinates without really understanding the needs and behaviors of people at work. By presenting motivation as some sort of theoretical, generic, conceptual subject for an hour or two, trainers broadcast the message that motivation is some abstract and unimportant area of human knowledge. Managers, for their part, have for several decades talked about areas such as motivation as "soft" stuff—squishy, spongy.

Both trainers and managers seem unaware that thanks to the research into the behavior of people at work that has been going on since the Hawthorne studies of the late 1920s, we have a firm grasp of what makes people excited about their work. We know about everything we need to know. But my experience tells me that it is perhaps the best kept secret in the management training field.

### The Value of Management Training

If you were to ask most managers what they hope for from the management training given their subordinates, chances are good that you'd hear such phrases as the following: a program that their subordinates will find interesting, that will motivate them to improve, about which they will be enthusiastic, that will be relevant in the real world, and from which there will indeed be lasting change in the management trainee.

The harsh reality, in this less-than-perfect world, is that most management training is interesting only to newly promoted supervisors and managers. More experienced trainees tend to develop a cynicism about the value of such training. For the new manager, the training is welcome because it is different from what he or she has experienced before. It's also evidence that the manager has indeed climbed that higher rung.

Interest in management training in the more experienced manager often has more to do with where the sessions are held than what they deliver—Florida in the winter, California, or New York City. With absolutely no intention of disparaging the programs of the American Management Association, I can testify that executives have told me through the years that they send their better performing subordinates to AMA's headquarters as much to give them a few nights in New York City as for whatever learning may occur.

*How Soon They Forget.* As we continue to talk about harsh reality, probably few managers see lasting change in the trainees when they return to the work scene. It's doubtful that more than a few see even short-term improvement in their subordinates. The impediments to useful change start in the classroom. Many trainees question the relevance of what they hear. Trainees are accustomed to hearing their charges say, "Well, this sounds good, but it really wouldn't work on the job." And when you don't hear such a challenge, you can bet that a lot of trainees are thinking it. Actually, the content of the program may be quite valid and could be usefully applied. But if trainers don't help the trainees to make the link between the classroom and what the trainees perceive as the real world, not much learning will take place. As I have often expressed it, the sooner the trainer can get rid of the walls of the training room, the sooner the trainees will be receptive to learning.

Are the trainees motivated to apply the learning and therefore to improve their performance? Motivation exists when a person says, "If I do such-and-such, I'll get the goodie I want." It's a rather unscientific way of putting it, but the fact is that people are motivated to achieve goals that they consider valuable to them—when they obtain a reward for the effort, in other words. What do I get, the trainee asks, if I start delegating more, or communicating better, or organizing my meetings more tightly? Is it worth the trouble to do these things? Will my boss take notice? If the trainee doesn't see a clear gain from practicing what has been preached, he or she will likely look at the new techniques or skills as something that would be nice to do "if I have the time, get the chance, and if people will let me."

We should not surrender too quickly to cynicism; many

trainees do leave the session with every intention to apply what has been learned. But the demands of the day-to-day work, the fires they must put out, the lack of encouragement or reinforcement by higher management all serve to dampen good intentions. What they return to is very much what they left, and soon, in many cases, the management they practice very much resembles what they did before the training.

Learning that is not applied soon disappears. It may be more accurate to say that learning that is not applied is not learning. It's very easy for trainers and managers alike to believe that learning takes place in the classroom, but I would suggest that it only takes place on the job when it is applied. A certain amount of forgetting what went on in the session occurs almost immediately. At the end of a month, perhaps between 25 and 50 percent slips away from us, and by the end of three months, most of it has been relegated to the brain's dustbin, unless, of course, it has been applied and practiced conscientiously.

*Putting Training into Context.* The lack of application is not the only factor in the forgetting process. We unwittingly accelerate that process in the ways we deliver the training program. For example, many management training programs come in bits and pieces. Trainees get perhaps two days of delegation, three days of conflict resolution, a day of communicating, a day and a half of interviewing, two or three days dealing with the problem employee, and so on. The inner logic in such a progression of what I call skills packages is hard for the trainee to see. Or the opposite approach may be used: a concentrated, all-at-once package. One manager wrote an article a number of years ago for the *Wall Street Journal* expressing his frustration over the six weeks' training he had recently emerged from: He couldn't remember which of the many solutions he had been exposed to fit which problem.

When skills packages are presented without a context or a perspective, there are at least three unfortunate consequences. The first, as I've already suggested, is difficulty in remembering. Context is very important in retaining knowledge. I'll use an analogy most people can identify with. You probably studied the American Civil War when you were in school, and during the process, you had a lot of names, places, battles, and dates thrown at you that you tried to learn out of context. Today, you have a vague sense of Shiloh, Chattanooga, Vicksburg, the Wilderness, Spotsylvania, Petersburg, and finally Appomattox. But when did they happen, and where do they fit? The appropriate context is General U. S. Grant. In 1862 and 1863, Grant drove south in the western part of the Confederacy to free the Mississippi from Southern control and to render that end of the Confederacy relatively impotent in waging war. So you have Shiloh in Tennessee and Vicksburg in Mississippi. Once Grant achieved that goal, he moved east to Chattanooga, where he launched one side of a pincers movement against the Atlantic states of the South. Sherman's taking of Atlanta and the march to the sea followed. Grant then assumed direction of the Army of the Potomac and set in play the other side of the pincers, fighting Lee at the Wilderness and Spotsylvania, investing Petersburg, and finally exhausting the great Confederate general at Appomattox. Once you have the context, battles and places and dates are much easier to keep in mind. What relationship does delegation have to anything else that a manager does? Much, as we'll see. But it often is a skills package simply thrown out there by itself.

The second consequence of presenting management without a context is that, as in the case of delegation, managing appears to consist of separate functions, not necessarily related to one another. But to be effective, it must be seen and practiced as a system, in which one function will have an impact on others. Setting goals, appraising, coaching, communicating, and delegating have a relationship with and an impact on one another. To illustrate, how a manager communicates during an appraisal session may determine his or her effectiveness in setting goals and standards as well as in building the credibility he or she needs in giving other forms of feedback to employees on their performance.

A third regrettable consequence of presenting skills out of context is that the skills themselves may be seen as unimportant. We invite the trainee to spend two days with us while we train in communicating. He or she goes away saying, "Gee, that would certainly be nice to do." But since the skill is not obviously part of a system, and nothing else really seems to depend on the communication techniques, he or she may not pursue them. After all, what's the urgency? In contrast, if you were a supervisor having to endure a militant union and an antagonistic work force, you would find an immediate importance in a seminar advising you how to avoid grievances. Somehow, communicating, by itself, isn't compelling.

### Motivation as Context

I advocate employee motivation as the context. Very nearly every contact a manager has with subordinates has a potential motivational value. Employee motivation is the essence of managing people, the key to the manager's success. The very definition of a manager is that he or she gets things done with and through other people. People who are motivated to do a good job are far more likely to do it than people who are not. When employees want to perform well for you, for the organization, for themselves, they know how important it is to commit themselves to helping their managers achieve organizational goals. People who are motivated to work happily show up when they're supposed to, put in a fair day's work for a fair pay, and go home in the evening feeling pretty good about themselves and what they've accomplished.

It's a lot more fun and satisfying to manage a motivated work group than one that doesn't really care much one way or the other. Managers are the key to the motivating forces in employees because managers can make it more likely that their subordinates will find their work rewarding. (Remember, the reward determines people's level of interest in the work.) Managers can also turn their people off. In fact, most disgruntled and frustrated employees will tell you that they could do good work if it were not for management.

Now you can understand why I believe that employee motivation is the very essence of managing and provides the context for learning and applying management skills. The way a manager sets goals, assigns responsibilities and tasks, gives feedback, distributes resources, and rewards performance has an impact on employees' motivation. All these activities constitute a system of managing; they are not separate and unrelated functions. Delegating therefore ceases to be something that it would be good for you as a manager to do and becomes an essential part of the encouragement of employees' motivation. Delegation develops and rewards, provides growth and a sense of progress, all of which have motivational force, as social psychologist Frederick Herzberg demonstrated long ago.

*Bringing Motivation Out of Obscurity.* What I'm proposing has been a well-kept secret: Understanding and managing the motivation of employees should be the first concern of the manager and may bring the manager more success and satisfaction than he or she has ever imagined. Yet to judge by the way managers generally are trained in motivation, you might reasonably assume that no one believes the above two statements. Motivation in many, probably most, training programs is at best a chapter in the book, sometimes only a section of a chapter. It is buried in another module, such as leadership or working with people. What is presented is usually generic or theoretical. That is: here is the concept; here is the psychology; here is the theory. Whatever the manager chooses to do with it may be left almost entirely to the manager.

*Frequently Used Motivation Theories.* Sometimes the theory isn't even useful and cannot be easily translated into practice—for example, Abraham Maslow's hierarchy of needs. Many trainers have told me that Maslow's is the theory base they use in motivation training, and I confess I do not know why. For those who may not be familiar with the hierarchy, Maslow ranked a number of generic needs. From the lowest needs, which are physiological (food, sex, sleep), a person moves to the next level to satisfy safety and security needs, then to those related to belongingness and love, then to esteem, and finally to self-actualization—becoming what one is capable of being. Maslow said that a person feels a particular need only when the needs lower in the hierarchy are predominantly satisfied, whatever that means. Thus a person probably won't seek the esteem of others until he or she has satisfied the yearning for belongingness and love. I doubt that. According to Maslow, need that has been largely satisfied does not motivate. I don't know how or when one has quite enough of love.

I don't know how to tell managers how to recognize the need that an employee is working on at a given time. It's an interesting theory and its publication made us all very aware of the complexity of people's needs and goals, but I do not know how to translate it into practice.

Frederick Herzberg's two-factor theory is also complicated but easier to translate. It does a fairly good job of explaining the motivation of people at work. The following, in Herzberg's research, have proved to be motivators: achievement, recognition of achievement, work itself, responsibility, advancement, and possibility for growth. I don't question these, but there are ambiguities in his list of dissatisfiers, factors that don't motivate but when absent from work create dissatisfaction. The list includes such things as supervision, positive working conditions, salary, and interpersonal relationships. Salary by itself may not be a motivator, but as a recognition of achievement, it can be. Supervision can be translated into a motivating factor if it is seen as a reward—in other words, greater accessibility to the boss in exchange for good performance. Herzberg's work validates much of sound psychology, but it isn't basic or simple enough for me.

## Expectancy Theory

For some years I have advanced the idea of using Expectancy Theory as the base of motivation training. When I started doing so in my talks with trainers, it was not unusual for me to survey a large group of HRD professionals and find that only a handful were using the theory; the rest were relying on Maslow and Herzberg. From my recent speeches and quick-and-dirty surveys, however, I'm encouraged. My perception is that more trainers and managers, too, are recognizing the value of Expectancy Theory.

There are excellent reasons for using Expectancy Theory as the basis for motivation training and as the context for most management training. First of all, it is universal—it covers everyone in every kind of activity. It is practical, as you'll see. The famous German-American psychologist Kurt Lewin used to say that there is nothing so practical as a good theory: It is simple; it is mainstream psychology; it has been around a long time; and the beauty of it is that it works.

Here is Expectancy Theory: Human behavior is a function of (1) the value of the reward that a person believes he or she will enjoy as a result of choosing a certain act or behavior or making a specific decision and (2) the expectation that the doer or chooser will be able to attain that reward. Let's use the simple example of buying a new car. You narrow your choices to three models. Your preferred choice is very sporty, has a number of exotic accessories, and has a very powerful engine. It is also rather expensive. The other two are more conservative, less expensive, but less impressive. You consider that the initial cost of your preferred choice will be quite high, as will the insurance and the expense of garaging it. It simply is not attainable, unless you are willing to undergo much sacrifice in other areas of your life. When the value of the reward is high but the attainability is low, chances are that you will choose a lesser value but a more realistic option.

In setting your career goal, you think that you might like eventually to become CEO of your company. But when you think of what you have to do in order to reach that lofty position, you may decide to settle on a lesser position. Expectancy Theory explains all of your choices, from your career to the responsibilities you seek to the tasks you select to start your day to what you will order for lunch. To remember the theory, all you have to keep in mind are these two questions: How valuable is the option? Can I realistically hope to have what I want from it?

***Building on the Theory.*** The practicality of the theory is immediately evident: Managers have the means to make the work more valuable for their employees and to help them be successful in doing it. It's that simple. Accepting this reality, we can construct the following five steps that cover just about all of the functions of a manager in dealing with subordinates:

1. Tell employees what you expect them to do.
2. Make the work valuable.
3. Make the work doable.
4. Give employees feedback while they are trying to accomplish what you want.
5. When employees have accomplished what you expected, reward them.

However, I must warn you. Like most "simple" truths, the steps are complex and difficult. Let's look at each and discover how you can build a whole system of management training and practice on Expectancy Theory.

1. *Tell employees what you expect them to do.* As a manager, do you sit down with each of your subordinates on a regular basis and agree on goals to achieve and performance standards to observe?

If you answer yes, congratulations. If you say no, you're in the majority. Why don't you? You get busy and forget. You may not have a clear fix on the goals. No one talks with you about them. Perhaps you have difficulty talking with your employees—many managers do. Probably the most usual explanation for your failure to conduct periodic goal-setting sessions with your people is that you assume they already know what you want. The way to tell whether you are right is to look at the performance of most of your people. If they are indeed giving you what you expect, if they are hitting your targets, you're undoubtedly correct in assuming they know what you want. On the other hand, if you have to admit that your folks are not performing as you wish much of the time, are falling short or missing your goals frequently, don't seem to understand the standards of performance you'd like from them, you had better stop assuming they know what you want.

Consultants in my business make a great deal of money narrowing the gap between managers' perceptions of what employees should do and what employees believe the manager wants them to do. A manager calls in a consultant to express frustration over the disappointing performance of employees. He or she may even suggest that the employees have lost their loyalty or the work ethic or have become rebellious. The consultant interviews the employees, who make it clear that they are puzzled by the manager's anger and coldness. The consultant then returns to the manager and asks, "When was the last time you discussed your goals and standards with your people? They think they're doing what you want." You can imagine the manager's answer.

The fundamental truth about human behavior is that all—repeat, all—human behavior is directed toward goals. Occasionally I hear a manager ask, "What do you do with an unmotivated employee?" My answer is: "You bury him. He's dead. There's no such thing as an unmotivated employee." If the employee is not working to help you achieve your goals, he or she is pursuing his or her own. If your employees recognize that they can achieve goals that are important to them—and we'll talk about some of those goals— through helping you to achieve yours, you're very likely to have committed employees.

2. *Make the work valuable.* Do you know what turns your employees on, what they really want out of their work? You can't answer generally. You must know individually.

As you'll read more than once in this book, I'm convinced that managers have little notion of their power to make the work valuable for their people. Value means rewards. Many managers think simplistically about rewards—they narrow them down to money. Since they have a limited supply of it, they shrug and say, "There's not much I can do," and they turn their backs on the enormous power they have to encourage better and better performance from subordinates.

There are two kinds of rewards: those generated from within the employee and those the manager bestows. I would suggest that the internal rewards are, for most people, the more powerful of the two with by far the greater motivational force. And I suspect that many managers, thanks to poor training, are insufficiently aware both of the internal reward systems in employees and how to use these systems to improve performance. To use them, you must know your people individually, and some managers don't like the idea. I'm not sure why, but I suppose that some don't want to get that close to their subordinates, or they fear that trying to find out employees' values and personal goals might be interpreted as an invasion of privacy. The former attitude is regrettable, and the latter fear is largely groundless.

What are some of the more common goals that people seek through their work? Satisfaction, achievement, and accomplishment are very strong in many people. They want the feeling of actually having done something measurable and/or tangible, which is why some manufacturing companies have discarded the assembly line in favor of assigning whole portions of the assembly to teams, who can see the results of their efforts. Maslow was correct in saying that some people work for esteem, their own and that of others. They like to be looked up to and respected. These are people who will often seek to carve out some niche for themselves, some area of specialty in which they are better than anyone else. For others, power is an end. A leading salesman I knew years ago strove to be number one on the monthly production charts, and one of his rewards was being able to call the president to task when he didn't like company policy and practice. The president listened.

Frederick Herzberg established through his research that growth is a motivator, a reward. My thirty years of corporate life have persuaded me that most people like to feel that they are better, more skilled and competent, more knowledgeable this year than they were last. In contrast to achievement and growth needs described by Herzberg, certain employees have what psychologists call high affiliation needs. They like to be part of a group, making their contributions to the success of the group or team and receiving approval from its other members.

The list of what people look for in their work is long and varied. When the manager understands what employees' personal interests and goals are, he or she can sometimes provide the kinds of tasks, responsibilities, jobs that make it possible for them to achieve what is important to them.

The other kind of reward is external. I'll say more about that later. Suffice it to say at this point that managers are often surprised in training programs to find that they have an enormous range of nonmonetary rewards available to them to give to employees who perform well. And the message that managers should try to convey to employees is, "Around here, when you do a good job, you are recognized."

3. *Make the work doable.* To be motivated, employees must find rewards in doing the work. They also must believe that they can be successful in doing the work and thus achieve the rewards. Otherwise, they usually experience demotivation. I learned this lesson as a young man. For several years, I was a group insurance specialist for a large life insurance company in the mountain states. My job was to help my company's agents sell group insurance and to persuade agents of other insurance companies and independent brokers to place their group business with my company. It was an

area of the country in which personal relationships were very important in doing business, and I was reasonably successful.

Later, I transferred to the New York metropolitan area, where I discovered that doing business required a different set of skills. The competency that had made me prosper in the mountains of the West was inadequate for the more competitive, impersonal environment of the Northeast. I began to suspect I would not reach my goals, that I would not be effective, and I resigned. I was demotivated. Interestingly, my bosses never understood the reason for my disaffection, because they never really tried to find out.

Some thirty years later, I still sense that many managers are not trained to determine that employees have fears about their ability to do the work, lack self-confidence, or recognize simply that they don't know how to do the job their managers want them to do. The manager assigns the work; the employee smiles and nods. The work doesn't get done, or at least isn't done according to the manager's hopes and standards, and the manager is tempted to believe that the employee doesn't care or has lost the work ethic.

Learning how to get feedback from employees is a trainable skill. Also, the manager needs to know how he or she can affect the employee's self-confidence and ability to view the job optimistically. Providing resources, adjusting schedules, training, coaching, mentoring, relieving the employee of other burdens all can help the employee feel better about his or her chances of success; all help the work to be seen as doable.

4. *Give employees feedback while they are trying to accomplish what you want.* In any of my workshops on motivation, this step, this area, is the one on which managers want to spend most of the time. My sense is that in no other aspect of managing do most managers feel so fearful and hesitant, even inadequate, and the evidence from employees is overwhelmingly negative. They tell of managers who never indicate when employees are doing well; who give no criticism until appraisal time, when they dump it all on subordinates; who give no criticism at all until they are angry; who blow up at employees in public and thereby humiliate them; and who simply fire employees without any warning or advance explanation.

Feedback is essential to motivation. You cannot manage effectively without giving feedback to your employees on their performance. If negative feedback is to aid in the building of motivation and commitment in employees, it must be given carefully, caringly, conscientiously. It must also observe certain constraints. For example, criticism should be given as soon as possible after the deficient performance. You should confine yourself to behavior, never discuss attitudes or motives. Your criticism should show the employee how to correct the failing performance or mistake. It should be very specific: "This is what is wrong. This is why. This is what you should do instead." And, please, no laundry lists of accumulated sins. You want to help the employee to be effective; you should not wish to bury him or her. Positive feedback follows the same rules: soon and specific. When you see employees working well for you, tell them how much you appreciate the effort. Be specific about what you like.

Appraisals should measure output, not input. It's all very well to talk about a person's cooperativeness and taking initiative and responsibility and working well with others and manifesting a desire to advance. But what does any of this mean unless it is measured in the perspective of output? What happens as a result of all of these admirable characteristics? And there should be no surprises; if the manager has established goals and standards and given feedback during the year, the employee should walk into the appraisal session with a clear idea of what the manager will say. Furthermore, the appraisal should be seen by both manager and employee as a blueprint for future effective performance.

The truth about appraisals in so many organizations is appalling. In some of my presentations to my training colleagues, I ask the question, "How many of you work in organizations that have appraisals?" Almost all raise hands. Then I ask, "How many of you train the appraisers?" Again, on average, perhaps two-thirds respond. And then comes my final question: "How many of you work in organizations that have appraisal systems that do what they're supposed to do?" This time, only a relatively few hands go up. "So what you're telling me," I say, "is that most of you are training appraisers to do appraisals that don't work."

Counseling employees who have severe performance problems is an absolute must these days, in our litigious society. If a manager cannot show that he or she has taken every reasonable step to try to help an employee correct poor performance, the manager may receive a court summons for discrimination or wrongful termination if he or she tries to get rid of the employee. The counseling process, together with documentation of other interventions, will go a long way toward showing that the employee was given every reasonable chance.

Through proper training in feedback, appraising, and counseling, managers learn that with care and proper technique many employees who are not performing satisfactorily can be rescued, can be turned around, can improve.

5. *When employees have accomplished what you expected, reward them.* I reiterate: Many, possibly most, managers have little understanding of their reward power. They do not appreciate the means they have of shaping the kind of performance they want. The first rule is: Reward the behavior you want, and don't reward the behavior you don't want. Through effective training, managers discover that they spend a lot of time reinforcing the wrong kinds of behavior and disappointing performance.

Managers often learn the wrong lesson. They hear that they must treat their subordinates equally; they must not discriminate. But my message is that managers should discriminate: People who perform well are to get special treatment. That's the only basis for preferred handling. Forget the plaudits for people who are always on time, work a full day, are never absent, don't cause any rocking of the boat, don't question your policies or orders—unless those same people give you the performance you want.

I'm a Skinnerian, and B. F. Skinner is what I preach. Positive reinforcement, shaping behavior, behavior modification—these are all tools for the manager's use. They are not manipulative. If you are open about what you want from the employee, if you are honest about why, and if you reward what you receive when it is what you want, you are, as we say, authentic. There is no manipulation involved unless you set out to deceive.

***What Are the Rewards for Performance?*** Tell employees what you expect them to do. Show them why it is valuable to them to do so. Help them to perform successfully for you. Give them feedback to keep them on course. Reward them when they have been successful. You can then look forward to the very great possibility that you will continue to get what you want from them. Remember that people do what they feel rewarded for doing. Make your rewards attractive and valuable enough, and they will work well for you. This is a fundamental lesson for all managers, one that we in the human resource development field have communicated rather poorly, I think.

Too many managers assume that if they don't have money to give as a reward, they have nothing to offer. In this respect, employees are usually far more realistic than their bosses—they often don't expect money as a reward. When money *is* used as a reward, many organizations give too little of it too late. For effective reinforcement, you should reward as quickly after the performance as you can, but most employees have to wait several months, and then for an amount that isn't impressive. Furthermore, they may see other employees getting the same amount, even though the performance varies greatly. As Gilbert and Sullivan put it in their opera *The Gondoliers,* "When everyone is somebody, then no one's anybody."

What, then, does a manager have to confer as a reward for good performance? Praise, for one thing: You have an inexhaustible supply of it, and if it is sincerely given, it will always be welcome. You, for another: Give them greater access to you—your confidence, your company, your mentoring and coaching. More responsible and interesting work. More independence over the work. Time off. A lunch on the company. Training to provide growth and new skills. The list is almost endless, and seldom is the bill expensive. All you have to remember is to recognize the performance quickly and specifically and you'll usually get more of it.

### Offering Modules in Context

Expectancy Theory provides the theory, and the five steps described above supply the application and practice. Together, they give us a context in which most management skills modules can be presented. The following is a representative list of such packages or modules:

| | |
|---|---|
| Motivation | Discipline |
| Productivity improvement | Handling problem employees |
| Leadership | Interpersonal skills |
| Coaching (for problem solving) | Negotiating |
| Coaching (for growth and development) | Training |
| | Goal-Setting |
| Communicating | Performance appraisal |
| Listening | Giving positive and negative feedback |
| Interviewing | |
| Delegation | Managing conflict |

Any experienced trainer or manager will recognize the above as subject areas for training programs. Some we can eliminate from the list because they duplicate the intent of the five steps: motivation, leadership, productivity improvement. All three are usually delivered as generic programs, as umbrellas for a number of skills. As I've pointed out, employee motivation is probably even more often a subsection of the other two, but because motivation is the key to productivity and to leadership success, to subordinate it to the other two is an upside-down perspective.

*Coaching.* Helping a subordinate through a problem is making the work more doable in the employee's mind (step 3). Coaching an employee on his or her long-term growth and development is usually seen by the employee as a reward, a manifestation of the boss's interest in his or her advancement. My sense is that such coaching is a potentially powerful reward that many managers overlook, possibly because they get busy. Other managers intentionally avoid this function because they fear the employee will be developed right out from under the manager. My rebuttal to that argument is that those who perform well will go anyway, eventually. Why not, through rewarding, encourage the employee to perform even better while he or she is still with you?

*Communicating, Listening, Interviewing.* These three skills are related, for example, when a manager wishes to give or get feedback. If the manager regards communicating as a two-way process, then he or she will see listening as part of communicating. Some managers may unnecessarily restrict the value of having interviewing skills to hiring procedures. But in reality, all three skills, taught together, assist the manager in goal-setting sessions (step 1); in determining what is of value to the employee (step 2); in getting the employee's perception of the doability of the work (step 3); and in criticizing, appraising, and counseling (step 4). We might also suggest their usefulness in positive reinforcement, which will be seen as a reward (step 5).

*Delegation.* I suspect this is often described to management trainees as a "should do." It may not be seen clearly as a strong motivational tool. As a result, the trainee returns to the work scene vowing to do more delegating when the opportunity presents itself, or when he or she can find the time. What often happens, unfortunately, is that the manager winds up delegating those tasks that he or she doesn't like to do and then usually to a few employees who are regarded as reliable. Effective delegation, however, involves pushing down responsibilities that are dear to the manager. Enriching an employee's job with such responsibilities makes the work more valuable. Delegating can also constitute a reward: "You've done so well with your usual responsibilities that I thought you might like to take on this challenge." Another consideration is that when you delegate and thus enrich, you provide new interest and excitement, which helps to overcome the boredom or burnout factor. A bored or burned-out employee will find it increasingly difficult to feel confident that he or she will do the job well (step 3).

*Discipline and Handling Problem Employees.* These are allied and both depend on good feedback skills (step 4). The manager criticizes deficient performance, notes it in the appraisal, and, when it persists, counsels, after which the discipline is usually applied. All of these techniques involve turning problem performance around. In most cases, the problem is one of motivation.

*Interpersonal Skills and Negotiating.* For years, with minor success, I have maintained that we can build interpersonal competence through training managers in negotiating skills that are based on the same skills that professional salespeople use. In Chapters Ten and Eleven, I set forth blueprints for this kind of training.

*Training.* Certainly training is a means the manager uses to help an employee do a better job, as is true of coaching. Not only does it make the work more doable, but, remembering Herzberg, training can be seen as a reward, a chance to grow in competence, possibly even to advance to a higher level of responsibility.

In contrast, training is often presented in negative terms, almost as punishment. For example, in such memos and letters from managers announcing a training program as "You are expected to report to . . . ," the manager imposes an obligation instead of opening the door to excitement and opportunity. One of the most egregious examples of this nonsense occurred in an assertiveness training program for managers that I attended a few years ago. The trainer asked each of us to introduce ourselves and to explain why we had come. Roughly half of the participants said they were there because their managers felt they were too aggressive. The other half reported that they were considered nonassertive. The manager who says to an employee, "You are not OK. Go get some training and get fixed" cannot expect much learning. There's too much resentment in the trainee. I cannot believe there was much "correcting" done in the three-day assertiveness training program.

Interestingly, a few weeks later my boss called me into her office and suggested that I might want to take a university-sponsored public speaking seminar. At the time, my job didn't require much of that skill, but she said, "It might be useful to you some day." I viewed the seminar as a reward for my performance and was grateful for her thoughtfulness. And the skills came in handy mightily.

*Goal-Setting.* I recommend that setting goals be part of the performance appraisal. People should know what is expected of them. People should, as they say today, "buy into" the manager's goals and standards. The evaluation of their performance should be based largely on how well they have accomplished what they agreed to and what was expected. Also, the goal-setting session is a marvelous way to communicate periodically the manager's expectations (step 1).

I'm very disappointed that managing by objectives (MBO) is not more widely used as a basis for performance evaluation, because it offers so many opportunities for managers and employees alike. There are routine goals, which are an extension of what the employee is already doing ("You produced 200 units per month. How do you feel about 220 for the coming year?"). There are also problem-solving goals ("How can we get the error rate from 7 percent to less than 3?"). You might want to set an innovative goal—a new procedure, something that you are not doing now that would constitute an improvement. And don't forget what is so often forgotten: the personal development goal. What is the employee doing to grow, to become more competent, to develop? Specific action plans—a course, a degree, job rotation, an expansion of experience—should become part of the goal-setting process.

*Performance Appraisal.* This offers opportunities for the manager to clarify his or her expectations, to get and give feedback, to offer rewards, to add value to the work, to help employees increase their expectations of success through greater competence.

*Giving Feedback.* This module seems to be much neglected. Competence in these skills is absolutely essential in the management of motivation. Criticism can correct deficient performance, and praise can let employees know what you want repeated.

*Managing Conflict.* This module is relevant in step 3: making the work doable. If conflict between people or departments is getting in the way of doing the work, then there's clear justification for the manager to step in. I don't see training people in conflict management unless the conflict is seen as a performance obstruction, however. Conflict that does not impede the work is probably tolerable. In many organizations, there is an unjustified fear of division and disagreement. Conflict, partisanship, and politicking are always present in a vibrant, growing organization.

You've long since discovered my bias. The above skills should not be taught generically or in a vacuum. All of them can contribute to the enhancement of motivation and productivity, and that's the context in which I believe they ought to be delivered. When they are, there will be, I'm convinced, far fewer worries about relevance of training content and less of a radical dip in the learner's retention of the training, since he or she will find immediate application back on the work scene.

# ■ 6 ■

# Using Line Managers
# as Trainers

Asking functioning managers to deliver training is far from a new idea. My Orlando critic who said nothing is new is dead right on this one. I suspect way back in the early days of corporate training there were a lot of line managers doing it, because we hadn't grown many trainers as yet. Training as a career is a relatively recent distinction, as evidenced by the fact that most of us in it never intended to be. For a long time training was regarded in many organizations as a function of personnel, which is now known as human resource management. You'll still find some trainers who must report to the HRM folks, which does not make the HRD people happy. In the early days of organization development, specifically the late 1960s and early 1970s, some companies pulled managers out of the line to practice this strange new art, probably because we didn't then know how OD people are created. (Have we learned?)

I urge the use of functioning managers for yet another reason. I think trainers ought more and more to be consultants: diagnosing needs, prescribing remedies, directing training, and working afterward with the clients to make sure that proper development takes place. I might even be suggesting that good trainers are being wasted as trainers. In fact, some organizations have virtually removed trainers from the classroom, preferring to utilize them for working with clients to determine training needs, for follow-up, for team building, and for organization development tasks. In such organizations, the actual training is performed by outsiders and by line managers. I'm not suggesting that excluding trainers from the actual training is the wave of the future, but there's no question that their skills will be expanded to include consulting on the site.

### The Advantages of Using Line Managers as Trainers

Probably nothing creates more relevance, authenticity, and credibility in management training than the use of line managers to deliver some or all of it. Trainers often have to take time at the outset of the program to establish their credentials, especially in technical areas, to convince the trainees that they indeed know what they're talking about. There may be times when they never succeed, and rightly so. Many organizations routinely use trainers who have never managed to teach management. In such cases, when you have a classroom full of people who have come in from the trenches, you'll easily find credibility gaps.

*Giving Trainees More for Their Money.* Acceptance can come awfully fast when your audience knows that you've "been there." That was driven home to me back in the 1970s when I started giving speeches on a regular basis. As a managing editor at RIA, involved with various sales programs that we produced, I was invited to talk to a regional convention of salespeople in Hartford. I was given a standard brief introduction, but my introducer closed with the magic words: "And in addition to everything else, he's been there." Instantly, they were a warm, accepting group.

Indeed I had been there. I sold for the first twelve years of my career, and I've been actively involved in sales training ever since.

I learned the lesson well. Now in my promotional copy and biographical material, I make sure to include that I am an experienced line manager. Those "under fire" credentials have been tremendously helpful to me as a trainer. Not long ago, when I was doing management training for public-sector employees, I found they had a tendency to idealize the private sector and thus shrug off any of their inadequacies as managers by saying, "We could be good managers if we worked for corporations, but you can see that in the public sector it's nearly impossible." A few war stories from me about the private sector stilled that kind of avoidance.

When I give workshops on motivation, I sometimes get the usual resistance: "Well, it sounds good, but in the real world . . ." It doesn't take long for me to convince them that I have always lived in the real world, especially in those thirty years of corporate life, and that I practiced what I'm preaching.

Another common form of resistance these days is the grousing about cutbacks, poor morale, and top management's dumb decisions. Honestly, how could a manager really function effectively when the Goths are at the gate? Once again, in such a situation my real-world experience helps me to help them. I describe my last years at RIA, when my department was served notice that, in two years, we would all be phased out. Meantime, would we please continue to be productive? As directing editor, I encouraged my subordinates to jump ship and find a more secure berth somewhere else, if they had the opportunity. A few did, and that meant that the work load had to be redistributed as we took on the responsibilities of those who departed. Morale was virtually nonexistent, especially since top management seemed to ignore us and was uncommunicative. Yet for those months we maintained standards and productivity. Nothing slipped. We may have hated to come to work in the morning, but once there, we performed as we always had. Even in terrible times, a manager can insist on, and receive, outstanding performance. A trainer with management experience can effectively pass on this knowledge.

A side note: It has never been established that there is a close correlation between morale and productivity. I suspect most managers do not know this, because they seem so fond of talking about the need for high morale. Happy people do not necessarily perform better than unhappy people; all we know for sure about happy employees is that they are happy. I have always assumed, however, that when the conditions responsible for the low morale persist for long periods, motivation and productivity will decline. It just takes too much energy even to get out of bed. (In those final awful days, as I passed restaurants on my way to work, I began to think about lunch.)

I believe there is no substitute for real experience and exposure, no matter how intelligent you are. I have urged my professional colleagues through the years to be honest about what they can and cannot deliver. I once quarreled with a very bright consultant who had been asked to address salespeople in an industry in which she had been retained although she had never sold. She asked for, and received, a large amount of money for the speech, something she was obviously happy about. I asked her: "Do you think you were worth it?" She responded that they had seemed pleased, so, yes, she did. "Well, I wouldn't bank on it. Those people were all in from the field. You could talk principles of selling all you wanted, but you knew very little about their practice. You couldn't give them full value."

When you use line managers for training, you are much closer to giving the trainees full value. Textbooks are fine, and copyrighted training programs may offer much, but there is nothing quite like a trainer/manager who can empathize with a trainee's experience or problem.

*A Learning Experience for Line Managers.* Line managers can thus bring instant relevance and greater substance to training sessions. They can make the classroom walls disappear very quickly. Credibility and authenticity may be the greatest benefits to using line managers in training, but there are other benefits also. For example, as a result of their classroom experience, they are quite likely to be better managers. As any trainer can testify, you learn when you teach. Any time you conceive, design, organize, research, or interact with others, you add to your knowledge. I once had a colleague who wrote books on highly technical subjects. I asked him why he chose those topics. He answered that he had found that writing those books was the best way he knew to learn something of the field. My books certainly aren't esoteric, but writing them has reinforced the truth of what he said for me. It's an act of creativity and of learning.

Listening to others will expand your knowledge. Many training projects provide a concurrent course in listening skills. When the trainer interrupts questioners, or dismisses their questions, or answers questions they never asked, he or she gets forceful feedback. I find it necessary from time to time to give seminars and workshops where I can hear the perceptions and perspectives of others. After all, the best kind of training is really facilitating: helping others to open up, to share and exchange what they already know. It's too easy to play God when you sit alone and write. After a time, you begin to believe that you are a fountain of pure wisdom. A writer, like a manager, benefits from having his or her head adjusted from time to time.

Line managers who train acquire new skills and behaviors that will help them in managing. If they are to be effective in the classroom, they must be tolerant of the experience and opinions of others. Your way of managing may have been quite successful, you thought, but in a classroom, working with other managers, you find there are other ways to do it. There's a marvelous story about Johannes Brahms, the composer. He once heard a violinist perform his violin concerto in a very eccentric manner, quite unlike the interpretations Brahms was accustomed to. When the concerto was over, Brahms reflected on what he had heard, nodded, and said, "So, it can be played that way, too." Sometimes we "experts" have the same revelation in the classroom.

Of course, your line managers are acquiring presentation skills, perhaps some writing skills as well. And they're sharpening their abilities to think on their feet—instant organization, a valuable ability for managing.

Your line managers returning from training stints will be more aware of the need for continuing development of their subordinates. Now that they've done the training, absorbed the content, learned to listen, and understood the potential value of the learning, they can take on the job of coaching and mentoring their people, or those in other departments under your jurisdiction. They have raised not only their consciousnesses but their skills levels too.

The training department might also discover that line managers who are experienced in training bring fresh perspectives to the task. They may be able to offer ideas, suggestions, changes that will help the training operation to be more successful in selling its products and more effective in delivering them. As a partner in the process, you could find that you have a valuable new resource in helping you to analyze your future training needs. You also are likely to discover that you have an expert in your midst, if the manager has trained in an area that is useful in your day-to-day operation. "Go ask Joe about that," you can say.

## Overcoming the Negatives

But there's the other side of the coin. Most line managers recruited for training assignments lack some of the skills, such as presenting and designing a program. They may also be short on content. These drawbacks are rather easy to overcome; there are plenty of train-the-trainer programs offered today to help people acquire the requisite skills. And if your organization is using line managers for training, it's relatively easy to organize your own such programs. Most likely they'll be working with a seasoned trainer anyway, who can coach and provide mentoring. In my view, it's a lot easier, faster, and more cost-effective to train a manager to do management training than it is to educate a trainer in management skills. And you can probably train line managers for less than it would cost to hire a specialized trainer. Considering the cost of outside trainers and consultants, utilizing your managers would hardly be more expensive. I'm not suggesting that you not hire appropriate trainers or retain consultants—they can all bring a desired strength to your programs. But I am suggesting that you may achieve economies over the long term by including your line managers in the training effort.

There may be some grumbling that a line manager is so wedded to his or her way of managing that the trainees will get a narrowly focused, highly biased perspective. This is a risk, undoubtedly, but it can be overcome in most cases by teaming the manager with a good trainer. Working together, they can widen the focus and open the manager up to considering other ways of managing. Of course, some managers will probably be unsuitable for the classroom and should not be asked to do what they are intellectually, socially, or temperamentally unsuited for.

Some managers are reluctant to take on training assignments because they feel that there is a stigma involved, that they will be pushed into a backwater, or that other line managers who are not diverted to training will streak ahead. You can see this fear in companies in which managers are assigned to training full time for a year or two. They have a real concern that when they are reassigned to a function they will have lost ground.

The proper way to address these concerns is to reward these managers for the training. You can overcome their worries that the training department is a wimpy assignment or a backwater by creating prestige for the task. Make sure that the manager receives visibility throughout the organization and especially at the top. Announcements, articles in the house organ, congratulatory memos on the manager's success all help. Visibility and name recognition in the organization are a powerful currency. Publicize the favorable feedback from the trainees who laud the manager's work in the classroom. If the manager has suggestions that might improve the programs, see that they also find their way to higher management. If the manager is a specialist in an area, or becomes one through the training assignment, make sure that everyone understands that this person has expertise and can be a resource for others who need it.

If you are the manager's boss, encourage him or her by reinforcing the notion that this is a valued responsibility and you prize him or her for taking on the responsibility. Find ways of assuring the manager that you are not going to squeeze him or her out of the department or the job while he or she is involved with training. And find ways to recognize and reward the good effort, the successful training assignment.

Full-time assignments add another dimension to the worry of the manager called on. If I am out of the line for a year or two, he or she thinks, will I lose my competitiveness? Will I be overlooked or forgotten? (Some managers who take overseas assignments have shared this concern.) If you are going to divert managers for training, you must see that when they emerge they get jobs, responsibilities, challenges that cause them to feel appreciated and rewarded. They must also feel that they are a notch or two up on the career ladder, that they have not been shoved aside or bypassed. Once managers begin to see the training duties as a possible acceleration of their career advancement, those temporary assignments will be highly coveted. And, of course, managers who win them will see the assignments as a recognition and reward for outstanding performance in the past.

## The Many Roles of Managers in Training

Your managers can fill a wide variety of roles, depending on their abilities and the training needs of the organization.

- *Advisory boards.* As I've already mentioned, some organizations maintain ongoing advisory groups in divisions or in the whole organization to study training needs, trends, approaches, and resources. Their recommendations can guide the training department and functions as to the appropriate design and delivery of programs.
- *Training committees.* As manager, you may find it helpful to have your own group overseeing the various training efforts. Your subordinates can assist you in making sure that the training department offers your people what they need and work with the training department on extensions, modifications, scheduling, and so on. It's generally a good idea to have someone overseeing the training to ensure that quality standards are maintained and that the program remains on target.
- *Experimenters.* Your line managers can test new programs or participate in pilot courses. They can also investigate outside programs for their usefulness in-house.
- *Orientation providers.* Whether your organization has an orientation policy for all new employees, you can certainly supply additional, focused orientation for your new people, with the help of your line managers.
- *Subject matter experts.* A manager might be assigned, after training, to present whole modules in a particular area, or pieces of modules, such as role plays, case studies, or technical lectures. As the expert, the manager may be assigned full time to the training department or simply participate on a part-time, as-needed basis. The manager can also serve as the expert in your own department, a resource on whom other employees can call.
- *Continuing development.* Training is only the first step. Your line managers can make sure there are continuing opportunities for trainees to apply the new learning. They can coach, provide mentoring, and make sure that successful application is rein-

forced. They can also advise you as to the advancement potential of the people they've been working with. They may have specific suggestions about new tasks and responsibilities or career directions for their charges.

- *Presentation preparers.* Even if they don't actually deliver the training as instructors, they could be a resource for the training department in preparing material on subjects in which they are knowledgeable. The trainers would then incorporate the material in their presentations and courses.
- *Self-development.* Some of your people may benefit from self-directed learning on the job. Assign a line manager to work with training staff to prepare the written, audial, or visual material that your employees can use at their own pace.

There seems to be no limit to the ways in which your line managers can provide content, support, and reinforcement in your training and development efforts.

*Managers as Facilitators.* Another training and team-building role that line managers can play throughout the organization is facilitating. This function increases in value in direct proportion to employee involvement, whether we're talking about quality circles, self-directed and self-managed work teams, or other forms of participative management. Certainly our organizations are moving to a more open, participative style, even if the pace is glacial.

Facilitating is pretty much what it implies: It makes whatever is happening easier to happen. A facilitator guides, encourages, persuades, and influences. The function is quite opposite to directing. (Southern Bell apparently has taken this role very seriously, according to John Joos, manager of seminars. At the time of my interview with John, Southern Bell had run 420 of its top managers through facilitation training. After the training, the managers went back to their workplaces to serve as facilitators in groups.) Whatever the issue, problem, or subject of the group discussion, the facilitator helps the group identify the issues or the agenda, set some expectations or objectives, and get the discussion going. He or she keeps the group focused on the issue, makes sure that everyone participates who wishes to, clarifies or redefines the issue when necessary, and does the wrap-up and summarizing. The facilitator must also be prepared to deal with obstacles to the success of the group, such as resistance to talk about certain issues, or people's feelings that get in their way, or participants' behaviors that obstruct progress.

Facilitating is an informal role. The facilitator does not act as chair. Some groups even do without a formal leader. I've seen facilitators do their work seated with the others around the conference table, or at the flipchart holding a marker, or seated slightly apart from the rest of the group. The facilitator is not there to join in the discussion itself, but he or she may ask for clarification of ideas and statements and write them down, even urge the group to decide on a solution or action plan. In short, a facilitator is in the group without being a part of it.

John told me that the facilitation skills training is conducted by line managers in groups of ten. And yes, there is resistance. Some managers feel that they are surrendering their managerial prerogatives; the threat is not an empty one. The move to facilitation must be strongly rooted in the culture and heavily reinforced by management. The message must be clear: This is the way we do it here—and will continue to do it. As more managers are trained in facilitation skills in an organization, the resistance will fade. Realistically we have to acknowledge that some people will never quite be able to shed their directing roles and will feel more and more alienated in such a culture.

It is a remarkable development when an organization chooses to adopt a more open, participative style through training line managers in facilitation skills. The benefits can be enormous in terms of creativity. When people feel encouraged and rewarded to contribute openly without fear of punishment or censorship, marvelous things can happen.

*The Manager as Troubleshooter.* There is another definition of facilitator, one more related to organization development than to training. In building a work team, or in removing some of the barriers that people in a work group have constructed against team building, a facilitator may function as consultant rather than trainer. His or her job is to help the members of the work group understand which of their behaviors are constructive (build an effectively functioning group) and which are obstructive (keep a group from doing its business). In this type of facilitating, the emphasis is on the dynamics among the participating people. What are the things they must do in their relationships with the other members to enhance the effectiveness of the group, and what must they stop doing?

Sometimes as a facilitator you find yourself deeply involved with the pathology of a group. Many work groups have existed and functioned for years without truly being a group in which the members subordinate their objectives to those which the group has agreed upon. When you see a work group that is open, is supportive of all its members, is concerned primarily with the success of the overall groups, knows how to encourage helpful behavior and to discourage that which is unhelpful to the group objectives, you see a genuine team. A team is not easy to achieve.

This kind of group facilitation requires more extensive training than the training role I described. In training, the facilitator may be, and often is, drawn from the work group. In organization development facilitation, the person is usually a disinterested party, a neutral person who can intervene in the relationships between the group participants. It is very difficult for such a facilitator to work with colleagues with whom he or she interacts regularly. There's too much suspicion that he or she might have a vested interest in a particular outcome of the group. The goal of the group facilitator is rather to help the participants decide on a solution or decision that *they* regard as best. Such facilitation requires extensive knowledge of organizational behavior, the behavior of people in groups. But there is no inherent reason why line managers cannot be trained to act as OD consultants to groups with which they are not involved or connected.

### The Critical Mass

Often in my discussions with HRD professionals, I hear the term *critical mass*. They understand that there must be a critical mass if major change is to take place in a corporation. There is no realistic way that the training department, or even the whole human resource management and development group, can successfully launch a systemwide change effort. The functional management must be involved, must support the campaign, must work in partnership with the HR people to get the job done—top to bottom, side to side.

# ■ 7 ■

# Providing Experiential
# Learning and Reinforcement

Training may occur largely in the classroom, but the true development part takes place on the work scene; the learning emerges there, through application and feedback. There's a strong message here for managers. Remember the basics of adult learning: People need to apply what they learn and get feedback on how well they do; they need monitoring and coaching. And I doubt whether any trainer, consultant, or line manager will say to me with a straight face that most managers today provide experiential learning opportunities on a regular, conscientious basis for their supervisory or managerial subordinates, especially after classroom training.

Way back in the early 1970s, I was writing that our corporations are learning laboratories. (*Laboratories* was an in word in those days when we were experimenting with sensitivity training and encounter groups and the instrumented labs.) I still cherish the hope that managers everywhere understand the reality that the best learning is real life and real time. But, of course, we HRD professionals need to know how to work closely with our clients to help them provide subordinates with such experiential learning. They need coaching and feedback skills. They must also know the difference between inputs and outputs, the means and the end, the activity and the results. As I've said so many times, ours does not seem to be a results-oriented society.

I suspect that the greatest waste of training dollars occurs at this stage: applying the learning. The manager who pays the bill should act to protect his or her investment. But managers get busy, or they mistakenly believe that the learning process occurs predominantly in the classroom, or they expect the trainee to take charge of his or her continuing development.

You *are* busy. The necessary groundwork *should* have been done in the classroom. And the trainee *should* supervise his or her development. But you are needed: You may have to provide opportunities for practice; you certainly are the one who will reward the successful practice; and, if you are to reward, you need to know that it has indeed occurred.

Ideally, a triple effort is involved at this stage: by you, the trainee, and the training department. First, the trainer has presumably asked the trainees to develop an action plan before leaving the course. To illustrate, if the program centered on delegating practices, the trainee would be expected to be thinking about what kinds of tasks and responsibilities to push down, how to identify the people who should get the added responsibilities, and how to monitor their progress. And you must monitor the progress of the delegator.

You have the learning contract that you've established before the course. If you're not sure exactly what was covered, talk with the training department. Then sit down with the newly returned trainee (emphasis on *newly*). Your talk with your subordinate manager should take place soon after the person comes back, when the course content is still fresh in his or her mind. Just as important, you convey the message that the training is high priority, not something that you will eventually get around to.

What happens now? That's what you want to know. Invite the trainee to tell how he or she plans to fulfill the learning contract. There are several things you listen for. First, does the supervisor or manager really understand the course content, the new skill, the new knowledge? Second, does he or she agree with you on the importance of the conscientious application? Third, is the action plan itself realistic? It's wonderful to see a trainee turned on by the prospect of demonstrating a new skill, but it's important to keep the practice within reasonable limits. Is the action plan doable in the context of the manager's total responsibility? Remember that goals motivate when they are seen as attainable. If the trainee finds out that they are too ambitious, goals demotivate.

Who's going to monitor the application? If not you, then someone else should be asked to oversee the postcourse learning. The trainee needs to know: Who will be coach and mentor? How will the trainee be evaluated? Will one new task be delegated each week, for example?

## Types of Opportunities

At this point you can see the fallacy of the so-called distinction between short-term and long-term priorities. Training and development are often seen by managers as long term, whereas the pressure is on them for short-term performance. But development is short term as well as long term. If managers insist on immediate application of the classroom learning, they soon have subordinates who are more effective supervisors and managers. It's not an academic issue. The manager who starts delegating on return to the workplace is doing something very right. The manager who begins to communicate goals and standards regularly to employees is on his or her way to getting more results from them. The manager who now knows how to criticize employees' poor performance without demotivating and angering them will see changes quickly. It's nonsense to say that developing your subordinates is a long-term matter and must play a secondary role in favor of short-term results.

*Follow-Up.* If the training department is on top of things, it should be in touch with you and with the trainees. Nancy McGee says that at C&S Georgia Corporation the department seeks feedback from the trainees thirty to sixty days after the course ends. That sounds about right. But I think that the training department ought also to check with the trainees' managers to get their inputs on how the learning is being applied and what kinds of results they are getting. The contact serves also as a reminder to the managers that they should be paying attention. The trainers should ask both managers and trainees such questions as "What is being used from the course?" "How is it being used?" "How successful is it?" (If it isn't successful, why isn't it? Is it the trainees' problem or should the course be modified?) The old-fashioned notion that the training department's responsibility ends when the course is over and the evaluation sheets are analyzed is self-defeating. Trainers as well as the trainees and their bosses must carry accountability for the success or failure of the development.

Some of the trainers whom I interviewed offer their companies' approaches to following up the classroom training with experiential learning:

*Cross-functional assignments.* Don Begosh of Lever Brothers says they feel it is important to provide managers in one function with experience in another. A financial manager might find himself or herself assigned for a time to a very different function, such as marketing or production. At Citizens and Southern Corporation, Carol Phillips describes cross-functional teams that tackle various kinds of problems that also cross lines of authority, such as quality improvement. At Aetna Life and Casualty Company, some managers rotate between jobs, according to Badi Foster.

*Special projects.* Aetna also provides assignments to special projects, with the manager being coached by his or her boss, another executive, or someone brought in as a third party.

*Faculty.* Sue Thompson at Levi Strauss & Company plans to use functional managers as faculty for future Leadership Weeks at which the company's management looks ahead to ask such questions as "What do we need to be successful in the 1990s?" At Levi Strauss also there has been for some time a quality enhancement program using teams or quality circles. They started at the top and are working their way down. Many companies have had varying and disappointing experience with employee involvement primarily because they didn't prepare the culture. Managers can get quite nervous about quality circles and their managerial prerogatives when they haven't been involved themselves, top down.

Karen Kolodziejski of Tektronix Inc. reports that her company has a train-the-trainer program to enable people within the organization—specialists and managers—to train others in the company. As I have already mentioned, it's usually cheaper to train a manager to be a trainer than to train a trainer in how to manage. There's a lot more credibility in an experienced manager helping other managers to deal with their real-life problems in the seminar, and using functional managers in training is an effective way to broaden their prespectives, to expose them to new knowledge and different ways of managing.

*Mandatory coaching.* Some companies don't leave coaching to chance. At CVS, Mal Warren says that managers are expected to coach the newly returned trainee once a week until the manager is satisfied that the new behavior becomes regular for the trainee. In some organizations, the training department follows up the training by asking the trainee how he or she is using what was taught in the classroom, and by following that up with the person's manager: "How have you seen him or her using it?"

*Task forces and teams.* Jim McMillin of Bull Worldwide Information Systems is an advocate of task forces that tackle strategic problems that cross boundaries. Later in this chapter I talk about the value of using task forces to develop your managers, which is a remarkably effective tool. But almost any kind of team, especially the leaderless variety, can help managers learn how to solve problems and make decisions collaboratively. They can put to work all those wonderful things they learned in the classroom about their relationships with others at work.

*Mentoring.* Dianne Heard, an OD consultant with about ten years' experience inside as a corporate trainer, believes in a strong mentoring system for the development of managers after training. These days some companies are formalizing mentoring programs to make sure that their developing managers get the guidance and counsel that will help them. It's more than simply a matter of pairing people. There are a number of factors to consider: chemistry, tolerance of the mentor for different ways of doing things, rewards for successful mentoring. Nevertheless, mentoring is in my opinion a potentially excellent approach to continuing development on the job.

*Action teams.* When Jack Dreyer (now of Wakefern) was at St. Regis Corporation (now part of Champion International, Inc.), he experimented successfully with what he called action teams, in which managers and supervisors held sessions in their own departments as part of an organization improvement effort. The plant manager met with teams of supervisors and managers to work on real problems, often the cross-functional variety. The managers also held round-table discussions with their subordinates to collect data about the operation that could be useful in action-team meetings and to communicate the results of those meetings. Not only did the action teams solve real problems and recommend improved techniques but the members improved their own skills in listening, making presentations, and learning how to work better with others.

*Feedback—Before and After.* Providing "before" and "after" feedback can be very effective in training as well as in evaluating the results of training. Before the course, you invite the training department to solicit opinions about the trainee's performance or behavior from those who work with him or her. They might describe a person who communicates poorly, who is brusque and abrasive, who listens only sporadically, or who seems arbitrary and insensitive in giving feedback. During the course, the trainee has this information fed back to him or her. Usually the trainer will have a one-on-one session with the trainee: "This is how your subordinates (or your co-workers, or your bosses) see you. How do you account for their perceptions?" Such intimate feedback not only breaks down resistance to the training but provides a specific direction for the trainee to take.

After the course, when the trainee has had sufficient time to practice new behaviors, the training department again surveys the same people with the same questions. Again, the information is fed back to the trainee. If the new behaviors are successful, the post-course survey provides encouraging reinforcement. And, of course, the feedback constitutes an evaluation of the success of the program or intervention.

It's a good idea to make another survey some months later to ensure that the changes in behavior or techniques have indeed taken root. Once again, the survey information can guide the trainee and reinforce the changes.

*Task Forces as Developers.* Development should be ongoing and doesn't have to be focused on a training course. The mentoring and coaching continue. One excellent management development tool that is still underutilized after all these years is the task force.

A task force is not a committee. Generally, a committee is formed to investigate and to advise; a task force is not usually formed to advise management but rather to do something, to run something, to make a decision. A committee operates for someone else who has responsibility. A task force takes responsibility and therefore often enjoys a higher level of authority than that accorded to its members individually.

There are other important and distinguishing characteristics of the task force. It is usually interdisciplinary or interfunctional. A chemist might sit with an accountant or a machinist; a marketing manager might deliberate with a computer programmer. Or the members may be essentially of the same level but from different departments. It isn't necessary for everyone to be at the same level. Diagonal slices work well, as long as everyone on the task force accepts the reality that the only authority that matters in the conference room is that of the group as a whole. People from diverse backgrounds and different functions can create dynamics that people who work together constantly cannot. They bring a different perspective to a problem that may have plagued a department or organization for years.

The task force normally is a temporary problem-solving or project-starting group, either full or part time. It therefore has a beginning and an end. If a new department or operation results from the work of the task force, it is common practice to turn over its leadership to a permanent management group, some of whose members come out of the task force.

For a developing supervisor and manager, the task force can be a splendid learning experience. I've never understood why it has been so underused. Twenty years ago some of us were touting the advantages of the task force to solve problems, to launch new projects, to devise strategies, even to reorganize a company. The most successful product I was ever involved with was created by a task force. While I was a young editor at RIA, we needed to define a weekly publication that went to middle managers, because we had been sending a hodgepodge with no discernible direction. We brought together a lawyer, an economist, a salesman, a couple of management experts, and others to make a new publication. It took the part-time task force about five months, at which time the group was producing the new weekly report. Then, before disbanding, the task force recommended that a new department be established to continue the editorial production, even suggesting the people who should constitute the department—all three from the task force. The result was the *Personal Report for the Executive,* which eventually became one of the most profitable publications RIA ever put out.

The manager sitting on the task force can enjoy more authority than he or she is used to and can exercise that authority within the constraints imposed by the group and its charter. The manager can see how teams are built, because, if the task force is successful, he or she is part of a team. Members of the task force can sharpen their interpersonal skills because the group climate fosters collaboration. A manager can be part of more effective decision making, since the group will probably insist on consensus decisions rather than simple majority votes. He or she can increase skills in managing conflict, because a true group provides a supportive environment for working through disagreements. Other skills he or she can practice include running meetings, listening, mediating and negotiating, goal-setting, and organizing.

The task force can provide achievement, from which comes development. The group experience also provides the developing supervisor or manager with a model of a supportive team for emulation in his or her unit or segment of the department. You can employ the task force as a reward system. Art did such good work on a recent task force that you propose him now for a more complex, prestigious group. And of course Art's development continues admirably. You not only benefit from your subordinates' increased management competence but you may get some troublesome problems solved.

## Action Learning

Back in the 1970s, General Electric Company, Ltd., of Great Britain pioneered a concept that offers tremendous development opportunities for managers. It was called "action learning," and it had dual objectives: One, it was a way to spot middle managers with high potential; two, it gave them valuable practical experience even before they assumed larger responsibilities. Here are the basics of the action learning program. Successful managers in midcareer, chosen by their bosses, are released from their regular responsibilities for six to eight months. They are invited to become consultants to other divisions of the company, though their salaries are paid by their own group. Top executives of each client division suggest major problems that have gone unsolved. The visiting manager takes over one of these to study in depth, with these important provisos: The project has to involve a major business problem that will broaden the manager's understanding of the company (nothing strictly technical or minor); the problem has to be outside the manager's previous experience and specialty.

Four days a week the visiting consultant works alone on the project—observing, gathering data, interviewing people. But on the fifth day, the manager joins four others who are also in the program, all working on different problems in other divisions, all with different backgrounds. Also present is an experienced consultant, from within or outside the corporation, whose know-how the group, called a "set," can draw on. Here, at the day-long weekly meeting, each manager brings the others up to date, using their ideas to work out recommendations to the client division. Each member of the set also receives feedback, positive and negative, on his or her work methods in the client division. Toward the end of the six-to-eight-month period, senior management also meets with each set to listen and comment. The goal of the program is for each visiting manager to suggest how to eliminate the problem assigned and, if time and responsibility allow, to start to put into effect the proposed solution.

*Minuses and Pluses.* A drawback may be that what goes on in the client division is discussed in the set, so the division manager may have problems with an outsider seeing problems that haven't been solved. In addition, the program is costly: The manager's own division is paying his or her salary without having the benefit of the manager's services.

The benefits, on the other hand, are many. The company and the client divisions benefit from having managers already familiar with corporate policies and practices devote full time to a sticky, serious problem. A visiting manager, especially one from a different specialty, brings a fresh point of view, can dig where it might not be wise for an insider to probe, has no political ties, and has no preconceptions about what's wrong (and who is to blame). Managers who go through the program learn the value of cooperation, of the team approach. They also learn to reexamine their habits of mind, become more receptive to others' solutions, and understand the wisdom of not accepting givens and of listening to people on all levels. They acquire new skills as well as confidence in their ability to diagnose and resolve problems.

*Adapting to Your Own Company.* You don't have to be a General Electric Company to adapt this concept. No doubt you can find opportunities and problems for some of your developing managers to work on as a consultant. You don't have to do without them for as long as six months. You do, however, have to back your consultants fully; they must know that they have your support wherever they are visiting.

## Immediacy Is the Key

Whatever the developmental approach you use with your subordinate managers, you'll be well advised to observe the following realities as soon as possible after training.

1.  Decide on how the trainee is going to apply the learning. Your interview with him or her should take place as quickly as possible after the end of the course.
2.  Provide assignments that offer opportunities for application. Make sure they challenge and stretch the trainee moderately. Don't push the trainee to the breaking point.
3.  Monitor the application of the new learning until the trainee is familiar and comfortable with it and until the new behavior is established. Give feedback as necessary. The feedback should be timely—that is, it should follow the application or practice soon.
4.  Recognize the success of the application. Praise the trainee for the accomplishment of making the new behavior a part of him or her.

# ■ 8 ■

# Aligning Reward Systems
# with Training Goals

When today's managers finally catch on to the reward power they have, the United States ought to easily outstrip every other developed nation. Most of the senior trainers interviewed for this book could not point to direct reinforcement of the learning in their corporations. Clearly we need to rethink our reward structures. This is rather a new area into which we must move. Most reinforcement of learning that I've seen so far is through the annual appraisal, which may be too long after the application to constitute adequate reward—that is, even if the appraisal system is designed right, which in many, possibly most, cases it is not.

Writing about rewards given to people in organizations for their perfomance always suggests a paradox to me. Managers tend to agree almost without thinking that rewards are a good thing. After all, they've heard about rewards in all the speeches and seminars and read about them in all the articles and books through the years. It's standard management stuff.

But the other side of the rewards issue—and yes, it is an issue—is that I doubt whether many managers really believe that rewards accomplish much. Perhaps I could be kinder and suggest that their skepticism, or at least lack of belief, is rooted in their not really understanding what rewards can do.

I'll give an example of how people—sophisticated people—take the notion of rewards much like apple pie and the flag, not to say motherhood. A few years ago, I sat on a task force for the American Society for Training and Development (ASTD). The subject we were examining was "integrating human resource development (HRD) into business." Our task was to come up with recommendations for CEOs, HRD professionals, and ASTD itself to help them increase the impact of training and thereby strengthen the global competitiveness of American business.

During the brainstorming session to develop good counsel for CEOs, the ideas were noted on a flipchart. One of my contributions was "Align your reward system to reinforce the training." The idea, of course, is that if you want your folks to apply what they've learned, you should encourage the application with rewards. Everyone nodded, but the person in charge of the flipchart stayed seated. A few more contributions from others were noted on the flipchart. I thought perhaps I'd try again. "We should tell the CEOs to align their reward structure to reinforce the learning." Once again, everyone nodded sagely, but there was no notation on the flipchart. The third time around, I decided that some amplification was needed. I said, "You know, it is such a simple thing, using the reward structure to reinforce the learning, we probably overlook it." This time there was the nodding and also some people agreed with me aloud, "Oh, it is such a simple idea. It is overlooked." If anyone reading this is in suspense, let me put it to rest quickly. The notation was never made, and I never understood why. Perhaps I misunderstood how some of my colleagues that day used the word *simple*.

### Power to Influence

It can't be said more simply—meaning uncomplicatedly—than this: As a manager, you have no more powerful tool to influence the performance of your subordinates than rewards. Of all the kinds of reinforcement of learning you have at your disposal, your reward power is the strongest.

Do American managers really believe this? Look at the way

our organizations reward their people. The most common means of bestowing rewards is through some kind of merit increase, usually given once a year and usually in amounts that fail to convince employees that the increase is due to their performance. Several years back, the nonprofit Public Agenda Foundation of New York reported that its surveys showed that 78 percent of American workers do not see a direct relationship between how hard they work and how much they are paid. More recently, the Hay Group of Philadelphia issued a strategic research report for human resource executives that stated "only about half of middle managers and a third of your professionals feel their pay is linked to their performance." You can easily imagine how the rank-and-file think about monetary rewards.

During the research for this book, I asked the HRD professionals mentioned earlier how their companies rewarded the learning of their supervisors and managers. The vast majority answered that there was no direct link between rewards and learning that should lead to more effective performance. One, a long-time professional, who back in the 1970s when we liked to put labels on people and their roles would have been described as a Grizzled Old Veteran, smiled when I asked, "How do your trainees get rewarded for their learning?" and replied, "They get their reward in heaven."

That's a bit late. But then, the annual merit increase is not only late but often insufficient.

*Shaping Behavior.* No, I don't think that most managers understand what rewards can do to give them more of the kind of performance they want. And since I suspect that many trainers don't understand the link between performance and rewards, the message clearly is not getting across. Why? I think there are several reasons.

The first, and probably the most important, is that managers don't really grasp some basic tenets of psychology. All human behavior is directed to goals. Those goals must be seen as good. They constitute rewards. As we know from Expectancy Theory, people choose the goal that is most valuable to them, but they seek that goal or reward only if they believe that there is a reasonable chance to achieve it. Generally, people will not exert themselves unduly or commit themselves to an excessive risk.

As I pointed out earlier, many of our managers are not being taught basic truths about motivation. People will do what they feel rewarded for doing. Managers have it within their power to make rewards available. Yet often managers complain that their people are not doing what the managers want them to do. Sometimes, as I've said, it's because the employees believe they are already doing what their managers want, usually in the absence of proper communication by the managers. In other cases, however, employees do feel rewarded for what they do, and their managers gnash their teeth in frustration.

Take the case of an employee who comes to work late rather frequently. Her reward for doing so might simply be the extra time she enjoys not being at work. Or she gets the feeling that she is somehow special, and being late without penalty reinforces her image of herself. She might also sense that others admire her for her free ways. Still another reward might be her suspicion that her continuing lateness is driving the boss slightly crazy. The manager asks in frustration, "Why does she do this?" I answer, "Because she feels rewarded." "What do I do?" the manager asks. "Change the reward," I answer. General advice for all managers: If you don't like what your subordinates are doing, change their rewards. Make sure they feel rewarded for doing what you want them to do.

Years ago, when I was first learning how to manage, I received some excellent counsel: Reward the behavior you want; don't reward the behavior you don't want. If you abide by that simple guideline, you'll shape the behavior of your subordinates to your needs.

*Reinforcing to Encourage Repetition.* I sometimes believe that many managers recoil at such phrases as "shaping behavior," "behavior modification," and "conditioning behavior." True, the language was developed in laboratories where rodents and pigeons were trained to perform certain tasks, for which they were then rewarded. For example, the pigeon pressed a little lever to gain a food pellet. Instant reward. Or, as the psychologist would say, the pigeon's behavior was reinforced. Once the pigeon made the connection between pressing the lever and getting the food, the pigeon would try it again. The bird would keep up the behavior as long as the food kept rolling out.

Harvard psychologist B. F. Skinner long ago established that what works for his pigeons will work for people. As long as your employees receive rewards that they consider valuable for doing what you want them to do, they will continue to do so. Reinforcement leads to repetition. But you must remember to reward your people periodically for doing what you want. If the food pellets stop coming when the pigeon presses the lever, the bird will eventually stop pressing it. When your subordinates believe that they are no longer rewarded for pursuing your goals, they may stop and begin to seek achievement of their own, and their goals and interests may not parallel yours. When your subordinates return from the classroom to apply the learning, and when the learning involves developing new behavior or modifying the old, they want and need to feel rewarded when they are successful.

### Why Is Reinforcement Not Done?

*Worries and Objections of Managers and Trainers.* The realities are simple, but managers can be resistant; sometimes they suspect that what is simple won't work. But when it comes to rewards, they have other worries. The following are some examples.

*"All this talk of conditioning smacks of manipulation, or worse, brainwashing."* Granted, Skinner didn't sit down with his pigeons and carefully explain what would happen if they pressed the levers. But as a manager, you're supposed to talk to your subordinates about what you expect them to do. They should have a reasonable idea that when they do what you want, you'll reward them in some way.

*"Why should I reward people for what they're being paid to do? That's already a reward."* There are at least two straightforward responses to this kind of military thinking. One, when you reward the kind of performance you want, people know clearly what you want and want more of. Since you make the work more valuable to them, they are likely to continue. Two, most people don't regard their pay as much of a reward. Frederick Herzberg long ago established that pay is seen as a hygiene factor, not a motivator. That is,

the prospect of more pay when it's related directly to performance can be a motivator if people see money as a reward. If you assign an important project to an employee and say, "If you complete this successfully in sixty days, I'll give you a good raise," that may be a motivator. But in sixty days, once you have given the money, it becomes, as Herzberg argues, a hygiene factor—that is, if you take it away, it creates dissatisfaction, but it has zero motivating force.

*"My people know when they do what I want."* Well, if you believe this, good luck; you're taking a tremendous chance.

*"I can't keep rewarding people every time they do a good job."* True—and not necessarily true. When the employee is experimenting with new behavior, you want to shape it. For example, if your secretary turns in reports and correspondence with lots of errors, you insist that she take extra care to give you documents that are error free. Whenever she turns in an accurate piece of work, you compliment her. If she gives you a letter full of mistakes, you refuse to accept it until it is correct. After a time, when the behavior is shaped, is repeated, you'd sound silly continuing to praise her for what she does regularly. Now you want to maintain the behavior through intermittent reinforcement. Every so often, you might say to her, "You know, I can't tell you how much I appreciate the way you keep to high standards of accuracy." Or "I hope you take a lot more satisfaction from your accuracy, because you have every right to feel good about it."

Unfortunately, once the new behavior is in place, managers get busy and forget to reinforce or they begin taking the improvements and changes for granted. One day they wake up to find that old habits have reappeared, have replaced the better ones.

Assuming that professional human resource development people understand the principles of behavior change and conditioning perhaps better than many managers, why are they so often uninvolved with the application and reinforcement of the learning on the work scene? If this assumption is correct, the probable main cause is the dichotomy that exists between the training department and line management. In many organizations, trainers train and managers manage, but they do not collaborate in development. Trainers far too commonly see themselves as relatively powerless in the organization, with little or no influence on the way the line management operates. "Here's our turf, and there is theirs." That may be echoed on both sides of the fence.

Even in those organizations in which the doors could open to trainers to enter the line world and work with managers on the development of their subordinates, the trainers may not see themselves as consultants or may not have the requisite consulting skills to be effective in the real world. All that simply has to change.

*A Fascination with the Process.* A second reason why many people don't seem to grasp the link between rewards and results is that they unwittingly or inadvertently place too much emphasis on activities rather than results. You'll recall my dictum: Reward the behavior you want; don't reward the behavior you don't want. Much to my surprise, many managers and trainers seem to value busyness rather than what it should lead to. I've come to believe that ours is an inputting society, and I'm not talking about computers and word processors. We apparently understand inputs better than outputs. We see ourselves as an *efficient* enterprise, although for many years one of our most important gadflies, author and teacher Peter Drucker, has been insisting that we be *effective*. Efficiency refers to how things are done; effectiveness applies to what gets done.

Through my many years of active involvement with ASTD, I've endured endless sessions with my training colleagues while they debated what should be done, how it should be done, and how wonderful everyone felt about they way they were all working together. There seemed to be little time left over to actually accomplish something, but then it didn't seem all that important. Trainers, incidentally, can take inordinate pleasure in their designs for training programs. What happens as a result of them is quite secondary, an unfortunate reality that has caused those of us in the HRD field to suffer a loss of credibility with our clients. We have too often been concerned about the esthetics of the schedule and methodology without seeming to worry sufficiently about whether our creation accomplished what our clients wanted.

But I won't fault my professional colleagues exclusively. They often work in organizations in which the reward system celebrates what MBO guru George Odiorne called the "activity trap." If you look carefully at many performance appraisal forms, you'll note that they emphasize activity and inputs—for example, cooperativeness or working well with people, managing resources, taking initiative, and so on. What happens as a result of the activity? Rewards are often based on inputs such as longevity and following the rules. One large insurance company until recently awarded employees one half day of vacation for every month in which they had perfect attendance.

My message is not that we should stop giving rewards for longevity or for perfect attendance or cooperativeness but that we should make it very clear what we are rewarding. My preference is to reward results—only. I've publicly advocated that managers should create an elitist group, an aristocracy of good performers, who get the perks and privileges. There would then be no confusion about what is rewarded.

Candidly, there is too much fascination with the process. It's fine to have certificates hanging on your wall attesting to your attendance at a number of management seminars and courses, but so what? The best attestation you can possibly have is your boss's praise over how well you have improved performance through applying what you learned in the classroom.

*Belief That Training Is Soft Stuff.* Management training is still considered by many managers and trainers to be "soft stuff," as opposed to the hard stuff such as skills training given to computer operators or mechanics. There is still a pervasive belief that the principles and practice of management are squishy. All of these years in which we have promoted management training seem to have added up to very little in building credibility and authority. So the third reason I would suggest for not linking performance results and rewards, especially when they flow from training, is that many managers don't seem to believe that what goes on in the classroom has relevance on the job. Sometimes you will hear managers say that what they heard in the course is fine under ideal conditions, but of course who works under ideal conditions?

Assume that a manager has returned from a course on delegating. His boss drops by his office to ask him to take on a special, rush project. The subordinate says to his manager, "Well, let me get back to you when I've decided which of my people should take this on." The boss says, impatiently, "No, let's not waste any time. I want you to do this yourself. That way, I'll rest easy knowing that you'll do it well and on time." How long do you think the subordinate is going to take the idea of delegating seriously? He has just been given his first indication that his boss doesn't have much confidence in the practice of pushing responsible work and decision making down to lower levels.

Sometimes the newly returned manager finds himself or herself punished when it comes to applying what has been taught. One such manager found herself in an extremely embarrassing situation in a meeting she was chairing when two of her subordinates got into a conflict about the best way to resolve a problem. She had been through three days of a workshop on interpersonal skills, and she decided to give the two time to try to work through their conflict in the meeting. Regrettably, her boss, who was sitting in, didn't agree with her decision. His face got redder and redder and finally he burst in, saying, "This is taking up too much time. Let's cut through the BS and take some action. This is what I think we'd better do." That was that. No doubt, next time she considered putting some of the course's principles into action, she hesitated.

One of the most appalling contradictions between preaching and practicing occurred to me at the company where I worked for many years writing and publishing newsletters to help managers be more effective. In article after article, we advocated the superiority of participative management and consensus decision making. Yet I was interrogated by top management about our editorial meetings, which they had heard were conducted democratically. Each editor's copy was submitted to the whole department. In a subsequent meeting, all editors on the publication voiced their opinions about the copy, and the directing editor, who was in charge of the department, generally abided by the decision of the group. He or she might like an article, but if the group said no, it was rejected. The directing editor, however, did have veto power: If the group was in favor of an article that he or she felt was wrong and unwise, the boss had the final say, but I can't remember that it ever happened more than once or twice.

The two of us who ran our departments this way were rebuked by top management, who obviously felt that we were weakening the operation and their authority. Never mind that for years we on the professional staff had publicly advised our management readers to take this very route. It may have been all right for them "out there," but it was too dangerous a practice to be tolerated in our company.

Reward the behavior you want; don't reward the behavior you don't want. Why is that seemingly more honored in the breach than in the observance? I've given three reasons: Managers don't understand the power of rewards; they reward the process rather than the results; they don't see the relevance of training on the job. On the other hand, many managers obviously reward exactly what they think they want, and then they must wonder why the results aren't what they expected.

### The Real Learning

What we know about how adults learn—and children, too, probably—is that there must be application and feedback. Thus, the real learning happens only back on the work scene. In the long run, the quality of instruction in the classroom doesn't contribute as much to the learning as an early application of what has been taught, along with the success or failure of the application. If it doesn't work, the learner needs to know that and why; if it does work, he or she needs to know that and why: negative feedback in one case, positive in the other.

Positive feedback, of course, is one kind of reward. When you want maximum effectiveness from your positive reinforcement, you need to practice the rules of feedback. To help you keep them in mind, I've started them all with the letter S:

- *Soon.* Feedback has the greatest impact right after the application of the learning. The behavior is fresh in the learner's mind; he or she knows more precisely what was done than later when the passage of time has blurred the details. When you've been successful at experimenting, you appreciate hearing about it before much time has passed.
- *Specific.* The more specificity you can provide, the more the learner knows what to repeat. General compliments such as

"You're doing a fine job. Keep it up" don't provide much direction. Keep what up, precisely?
- *Standard.* It should be standard behavior on your part to reinforce the application of learning and the experimentation with new behavior. Sure, you get busy, and you may assume that the subordinate knows of your approval, but take a minute to comment on what the person has done well. That minute will pay off handsomely.

*Closing the Contract.* Just as you sat down before the training to discuss your expectations and to listen to the other person's, you must schedule time as quickly after his or her return as possible to discuss the learning. Where does it lead now for your subordinate? How can he or she build on it? What are the implications of the learning for others in the department? Do you want the learner to instruct others? Where might the new learning and behavior be applied in ways that the two of you have not discussed? Are there problems that lend themselves to be solved by new techniques? If the learning has indeed been successful, how can it be expanded? What new career moves are opening up now that the person has increased skills and competence? Learning should be regarded as a point on a continuum. It goes on. It leads to more learning.

For you, the issue now is that you must justify your investment. How much has the training been worth to you and to your department? How can you increase the return? Unfortunately, most of the trainers whom I interviewed acknowledged that the process and means of evaluation of the management training were simply not in place.

*Providing a Variety of Rewards.* If you don't have much money or a promotion to offer the learner as a reward, don't worry. There are many other ways to say "Thank you. I appreciate your effort." Here is a review.

- *You.* Provide more access to you, a closer working relationship, consulting the learner from time to time for his or her advice. If the trust level between the subordinate and you is high, your personal attention and concern will mean much.

- *More responsible work.* The learner has earned his or her stripes; enrich his or her job. How can the responsibility be expanded? What functions do you presently perform that you can push downward in whole or in part?
- *More training.* Offer training as a reward. It leads to greater satisfaction, more opportunities to achieve, and increased self-esteem. Perhaps it is time for you to do some coaching for the long-term growth and development of the employee.
- *Your praise.* Again, if the subordinate trusts and respects you, your praise of his or her newfound success will mean much. Praise publicly, if you can. If you can persuade your boss or higher management to join with you in acknowledging the growth and accomplishment, so much the greater impact.

And, of course, this includes nice touches such as a better office, new or more sophisticated equipment, the chance to represent or accompany you outside the office, an assignment to a task force or to chair a meeting for you—in short, any kind of task that will broadcast to the employee and to others in the organization that this person has become more valuable.

Don't forget another kind of positive reinforcer: more control over the work, more independence from close supervision, both of which are usually very high on any list of rewards that employees come up with. When you say to a subordinate, "I trust you. I know you want to do your best. So go and do it," you hand him or her one of the highest tributes you can pay.

Above all, remember: Reward the behavior you want; don't reward the behavior you don't want.

# PART THREE

# Tools for Implementing
# Effective Training Programs

The big risk in offering advice about training, of course, is the question, "Does it really work?" Yes, it does, and Part Three offers the evidence.

In Chapter Nine, I offer an interview with Karen Stein-Townsend, vice-president in charge of professional development of Johnson & Higgins, the large insurance brokerage firm. Her responses to my questions are ample proof of how a training program can be effective in the real world.

In Chapter Ten, I pursue an old cause: using basic sales skills training to enable managers to improve their abilities to deal with other people (interpersonal competence, to use the jargon). The realization that the very same skills that salespeople use in influencing and negotiating with their prospects and customers could be useful to nonsales managers came to me in the 1970s. At that time, as a member of the professional staff of RIA, I was advising our subscribers to the RIA management newsletters how to get better results in working with others: subordinates, other managers, their bosses. Although I was not aware of it for a long time, I drew my recommendations from my own training and experience as a salesman, which I was for the first twelve years of my career.

One day I experienced a huge AHA!, and since then I have been finding ways to adapt sales training to managing. My book on the subject, *The Persuasive Manager: How to Sell Yourself and Your Ideas* (1982), was hardly a success, at little more than 8,000 copies sold, but some readers later asked me to conduct workshops for their managers, using basic selling skills. Those workshops reinforced my belief that, as I expressed it in *Unconventional Wisdom: Irreverent Solutions for Tough Problems* (1989b), "You Need to Sell Well to Perform Well." The essay thus titled is addressed to managers primarily. Recently, Executive Enterprises in New York published a self-learning workbook, *Mastering the Power of Persuasion: How to Get the Results You Want on the Job* (Quick, 1990), which presents an overview of concepts and practical techniques.

I continue promoting my cause when I talk before management and training groups. Using selling skills simplifies the otherwise vast and complex area of interpersonal relationships.

In Chapter Eleven, I continue to urge that assertiveness training be made more common. Some of it is still around, of course, after it peaked in the 1970s. It is effective training in communicating, but with the addition of responsiveness, a development proposed by Malcolm Shaw, the communicating tool becomes a negotiating tool. Like sales training, assertiveness-responsiveness is a fairly simple body of techniques to learn. A knowledgeable trainer can design a good program in both disciplines for three-day delivery. Both programs, on sales and on assertiveness, can draw on readily available content and methodology, they're simple, and they're relatively inexpensive. Furthermore, as I can fervently testify from my experience, they work.

In Chapter Twelve I review the business world from the 1950s to the present and discuss its concern for efficiency and effectiveness. Once again I address the problem of our failure to attain improved performance through the training of managers. I summarize my recommendations to help trainers and managers increase the value of the training. I then take a look at the future, based on the cultural changes over the years, and at the growing importance of the work group in the new democratic organization. Our training programs must reflect this new reality.

# ■ 9 ■

# Implementing the Six-Step Program

I expressed some of the ideas offered in this book when speaking before an ASTD group in Manhattan, at the offices of Johnson & Higgins, the large insurance brokerage firm. After the talk there was what proved to be a spirited question time. Some of the questions from the trainers were probing and a bit skeptical, but to my delight, I didn't have to defend my thesis. William Whealan of J&H, who was our host for the evening, responded to the skepticism (it was rather slight) with, "Well, it works here. We're doing these things."

A day or so later, I called him and suggested that, since J&H was putting into practice what I preached, perhaps I could interview someone. Shortly after, he called back to tell me I could have an appointment with his manager, Karen Stein-Townsend, vice-president in charge of professional development. I had heard of Karen, but I hadn't had the pleasure of meeting her. On one of the last days in March, I sat down with this knowledgeable, articulate woman and asked her to respond to my six recommendations for more effective management training and development. Her responses follow.

A word about Karen Stein-Townsend. She graduated with degrees in both psychology and sociology; then went on to a career in social work, family counseling specifically, which she says she did not find rewarding. She had a more satisfying time working with Lawrence Munson of Louis A. Allen Associates, the management development firm. One account was J&H, and when she decided to make another change J&H beckoned, admitting that they weren't quite sure how they would utilize her but that she seemed to be the kind of person they wanted in their organization. The wisdom of that decision has been amply reinforced in the subsequent years, as you can see from her thoughts in the following interview. (**My comments and questions will be in italics.**)

*Karen, as I mentioned to you, I have been quite disappointed for a number of years in the way we produce managers in this country—or rather don't produce them. I have developed a six-step program, which I now recommend to management and training professionals, that I'm convinced will help us to develop managers who are more effective with people. The first step, on which I'd like your comments, is for human resource development people to establish partnerships with functioning managers.*

I believe in that partnership, but it took us a while to build it. I came out of human resources here at J&H—our HR department is separate from professional development—and because my career there had been spent helping managers solve problems, I felt very strongly that whatever we did in PD had better be along the same lines, helping managers, rather than using some esoteric guideline as to what training ought to be. What I had to find out was how PD could help our managers. Meantime, we canceled everything that PD was doing so we could start over again.

*What were some of the things PD had been doing?*

They were using outside vendors to provide a variety of courses, none of which supported or reinforced one another. None of the courses was really geared toward us and what we do. They were off the shelf: public seminars conducted in-house. The cost was extremely high, and the employees here were not really happy with what was going on. The managers didn't understand what was going on, but they weren't sure they were happy either.

My charge was to decide whether we needed the PD department or whether we should shut it down. I believed we needed it, but only as a partnership with the line departments, delivering what the managers there needed and wanted. So we literally closed down for a year. I spent that year visiting all our branch offices, sitting in on staff meetings, inviting myself to management meetings, and finally sitting down one on one with managers and just asking them, "If you were in my shoes, what kind of instruction would people be getting, if they got any? If so, how would it be delivered? Where would it be delivered? Who would be doing the delivering?"

*You were able to get good information out of all that?*

I got very good information. I certainly got a lot of tips on what not to do. It eliminated a lot of things that I had understood to be traditional in our training.

*Such as?*

Such as, don't hold the training courses in some central location and make me fly all my people to you. Don't give us the same course every time. Spend a little time telling me what I need to know about the course and what I should expect to see on the job after. Help me in terms of knowing whom to select for the training. Make the communications short and pithy but not so frequent that I stop reading them. But keep me informed about what's going on and find a way to make it easy for me to offer training to my people. And one more very important point: Don't charge me if there's any way you can figure out not to charge me. Because they all understood that when the economy got rough for us, the first place they would have to start to cut would be extraneous expenses not related to client work.

*Such as training.*

Training first and foremost. So I came back to corporate headquarters and talked to our COO David Olsen, who was very supportive of what I was doing. David and I agreed that the first thing we'd do is eliminate all direct back charges to the branches. For example, if you are the manager in Los Angeles and you send someone to one of our courses, you're not going to see an immediate charge of $412 or $2,000 or whatever. Corporate absorbs the cost of the training. There are no per-person charges to the branches.

*Is there any kind of departmental allocation?*

There is a minor charge that doesn't change, whether they use our services or not. It pays for the executive staff work at headquarters.

*Clarify this point for me. I've heard people who run central training departments say that it's really much less risky to insist that the various functioning managers have their own training budgets because if there is a squeeze on the corporate budget they say, "Let's cut out training."*

If the corporation believes that training its people is important, it ought to be a main-line feature of the corporate budget. I think also that asking each branch or department to budget for training means that you run the risk that some very needed training may not be identified until later when there's no money available for it. If it's part of the corporate budget, it's available no matter what they need. If they need customized work, they don't have to worry, "Gee, did I budget for all this?" One of the main ways for us to get back into their world has been to do customized work for them.

*Do you have a catalogue of training courses?*

We have a very small catalogue on generic programs, but in fact we probably do half again as many courses that are strictly customized.

*What are some of the generic courses?*

Presentation skills, maintaining writing skills, for example. We assume there is already some level of writing skills to be maintained.

Some communication stuff, basic managing for the first time, managing effectively.

*Real basic stuff.*

Yes. And those areas where we may begin to customize. Managing effectively is an overview course for people who have been managing for a while, but in an overview course you don't spend much time on any one subject. So out of managing effectively come twenty-one workshops, maybe two-thirds of a day specifically on delegation, another day-long session on performance counseling, or turning around a nonperformer. All of these workshops are customized and we deal with the local office to deal with their specific concerns.

Also, we work with them to help them resolve an issue. For example, in one office the management group was not functioning as a team. There was a lot of unhappiness with one another, some open rebellion in areas. We did a two-and-a-half-day workshop that we loosely entitled leadership and conflict resolution, but it was specifically geared at surfacing some of the things that were stopping them from working together and finding ways to resolve them. We didn't suggest ways. I really sat there facilitating and playing referee to keep them from killing each other and pointing out when they were communicating with hand grenades.

*How large a group was it?*

We had eleven people. It was a good size, and we were able to bring up a lot of problems that out of politeness no one had ever talked about with one another. But those are the very things that stop us from working together. Once they came out on the table, once they were named, they lost a lot of their power. We could then resolve ways of working around them. Everyone understood going into it that our objective was not to have everyone love one another and not necessarily to go out for drinks afterward, but to find ways of working together in such a way that as a management team we could meet the main objectives of the office.

*As I recall, one of the main problems we had with sensitivity training back in the 1960s was that in companies that experimented with it people found out a great deal more about their colleagues than they really needed to know or wanted to know. So where did the initiative start for this kind of work you did with the management team?*

The trust takes time. It really started with the initial sales work in that first year or two, when I just spent a lot of time listening. Managers saw that I wasn't out there selling my courses, that I really was concerned with their day-in, day-out problems, and especially that I wasn't carrying tales back to corporate. I didn't name names, and I didn't act as if J&H was a training company. Clearly there grew a level of comfort and credibility.

*That would take time.*

It does. That's why there was nothing coming out of this department for at least a year and a half, because I felt it was important to get the groundwork laid.

*Obviously you have a lot of support from the top for this type of venture. In contrast, in a company where I worked, they hired a trainer for a management training course. She interviewed all who were going to attend, and she heard a lot of sensitive stuff. There was no communication or trust top to bottom. Yet, when she held the three-day session, it was safe stuff like time management. I'm sure she would have risked her job dealing with the real issues. But some of us felt betrayed.*

Top management here is incredibly supportive of what we do. We have a statement of corporate purpose that is very highfalutin but the first line is that we are to be the best at everything we do. We can't be the best unless we devote ourselves to the only resources we have. We sell service, not widgets. If we don't devote ourselves to helping our people provide the best service possible, then we're talking out of both sides of our mouths.

*How do you and your people relate to the functioning managers in terms of who is going to do what with whom and when and how?*

We take time to talk with managers—in the ladies' room, in the men's room, in the lunchroom—nobody is safe from us. We want to know what they're working on, what they're involved with. We try to get ourselves invited to national practice meetings, for example, which have no direct connection with training. We try to be a fly on the wall to see what problems they have in their disciplines, what their world is.

Every person on this staff takes insurance courses, reads insurance magazines and other publications, and attends technical training seminars so we understand their language and what their problems are. In addition, we've gone to an account manager system here in the department, which is unusual for a training function. Every single branch has been assigned to a trainer here, and that trainer's accountability is to make sure that we are a working partner with them, that we have nothing but their own interests at heart, that we're not going to try to sell them anything they can't use, that we will only bring things to them that they can use.

We have developed a set of standards of accountability for ourselves in that account manager relationship that places the burden very clearly on us to be consultants in that process. Our obligation is to make certain that, if the branch is looking for a solution that seems inappropriate, we get our point heard. We can't, however, force a decision.

*If managers want a particular program that you know won't work, that isn't appropriate, what do you do then?*

We'll probably call them up and ask whether we can come talk to them about their objectives. We ask them to spell out their concern and why they were receptive to the program. What, we might ask, would be the ideal outcome? If we think there's another approach, we ask whether they'd be willing to listen to it. We're generally successful because we have credibility and we know their problems. Also, the one card we always have up our sleeves that outside people don't is that we live and breathe this culture. Because of our insurance focus, we can talk in their world.

If they insist on their own solution, we won't be obstructionists. We will ask permission, which is always granted, to be at that session and to work with the outside trainers ahead of time. We educate those trainers in the culture and the company to help them avoid pitfalls. Also, from our knowledge of the needs of the branch, we express some concerns, which we ask them to build into their program. By being in the room during the session, we can help when things blow up or when they clearly get off on the wrong track.

*Have you had problems like that where the manager had the revelation that this isn't so great after all?*

I can't think of a time when that hasn't happened, when they haven't said, "Karen, you were right." The temptation is to say, "I told you so," but I don't. I come back here and mutter it. Outside people can almost never deliver a program that is stronger than a good in-house program that is strongly geared to the strategic objectives of management.

*Let me play devil's advocate. Have you not encountered some highly specialized areas in management where you might find an outsider who has more in-depth knowledge even though the trainer or consultant doesn't have specific knowledge of J&H culture?*

I haven't found a need to bring in an outsider on the basis of subject matter but rather on the basis of the level of participants. There might be some messages that I think the board should hear, and it would be inappropriate for them to hear those things from me exclusively, if only because they might be thinking that Karen has a vested interest in this whole process. I also suspect that credibility sometimes is in proportion to the fees paid.

There might be some specific skills areas or disciplines that outsiders are more advanced in than we, and if so, it would be wrong of me to overlook that fact. It would mean there's an area of our operation that I'm not involved with. I couldn't afford that.

And I'd also want to extend my own development. So, yes, I would bring in the outsiders.

*You said that your people are prepared to go in as consultants. Are they trained in consulting skills?*

Not formally. However, we spend a lot of time in the department sharpening our skills. One way is for each of us to take the course that we teach and present it to the others in PD. We also videotape it. Then the presenter gets feedback, and it can be tough. The presenter may hear such statements as, "You sounded very tense," or "You seemed preachy to me," or 'You didn't give me a chance to answer the question." We're hard on one another, but in a caring and supportive way. We don't let anybody from outside the department sit in on these sessions. We evaluate whether we are listening, which is so important in consulting. We also have people on the PD staff who have consulting backgrounds, and we tap their strengths.

*On to step two, establishing learning contracts. Obviously you have a contract with your client, the manager. How about a contract between the manager and the subordinate who is to be trained?*

That may be one of the hardest things to get managers to accept, that it's very important. We're not as far down that road as we will be. At this time it's our practice to send a memo to the manager ahead of time telling him or her what are some of the things the employees will be taught in the seminar. We ask managers to make it part of their responsibility when the trainees come back to see how the learning can be applied on the job, and actually to look for evidence that it is being applied, and to reward it when they see it.

*But do they sit down with their people before the training session and discuss some of these things?*

We ask them to do that. We say, "Please talk to your employees about your expectations."

*And the employees' expectations.*

That's right. Frankly, I believe a lot of managers are still caught around the turn of the century in that they struggle with whether they have to talk with their employees.

*Even worse, do they have to listen to them?*

It's hard to get some managers to understand that that's something they need to do. We follow up the training by sending evaluation forms that ask them how the course can be improved, how it can be better applied in the manager's world. With lots of our courses we go back four or six or eight weeks later to ask the employees what they are using from the course, why, how, and we give that information to the manager. In a couple of our courses we actually send managers a sheet that the employees in training have filled out saying, "This is what I need from my manager in order to use what I have learned in the course."

*Do you ask the manager whether the employee has applied the learning?*

Yes, although in this we are not as sophisticated as we should be. Right now we're handling that mostly on a telephone basis and struggling with how we're going to be able to get this more formalized without its being a paperwork trail. But we want to know whether the manager believes it has been a worthwhile investment. After all, it cost the manager something in time and productivity. Has there been any change? It's informal now, but we need more in-depth information. But managers are very nervous that we might create a paper trail.

*Is there sometimes a tendency for employees to embellish the value of the training to them?*

Oh, I don't think so. J&H employees are brutally honest, and we get feedback we don't want.

*How'd they get that way?*

Our culture. Also, we in PD have built an extraordinary level of credibility. We say to people, "Tell me the truth. I can handle it. I'm not going to hurt you for telling me." We don't carry tales back. We don't report on people who behave inappropriately. And we may be training people, but our purpose in that is to help them with problems they have in work.

*We're not here to train you but to help you get the results you want.*

Exactly right. I should tell you too that we start off courses by saying that we'll accept any criticism you have to offer, but we won't accept your walking out of the room talking about what you wished we had covered. That is their responsibility, to make sure we do cover it.

*How do you individualize development? You have a number of people to be trained, and not everyone is interested in the same things or can learn at the same speed.*

It's very hard to do that in the workshop itself, and you can't slow the course down to the pace of the slowest person. You'd lose the others. So if we know that some people are struggling with a particular aspect of the seminar or have come forward to say "I'm having a hard time," we'll spend time outside of the session, at lunch, or before or after, and then we might also do a one-on-one follow-up.

*Let's say I'm one of your line managers, and I come to you saying, "I've got a couple of people in my department who are technically and professionally fine, but when it comes to dealing with people around them, they are awful. Can you do something about this?" What's your response?*

Well, we just went through that very situation. We didn't think that putting them in a seminar was going to help them, so we arranged a workshop just for them and us. We collected just enough information that we could talk to them about specifics of their behavior without beating them up.

*Did you get feedback from their associates?*

Yes, we collected some anecdotal information about what had happened. Again, just enough that we had something to work with. When the denial set in, we could ask, "What happened here? Let's take a look at the other person's perception of the incident." We were in a classroom but not lecturing. Instead we talked about the dynamics of their relationships with others, perceptions, and the validity or invalidity of perceptions. Over the course of two days, it can be very intense for them and us.

*How many people would you have in this workshop?*

Sometimes one. We have had two, no more, and they have to be from the same department suffering the same problem. In each case we made sure that the accountability for giving knowledge was on our part and for accepting was on their part. Also, we let them know what the consequences of their behavior would be if they continued. It would just be deeper and deeper alienation. That meant giving them cold and hard facts about the company culture. When you leave the room after those two days, you wonder whether anything has been heard.

*Did you find out?*

Yes. In one case, people told us that they had not known that we had a magic wand. The person had done a 180.

*What people told you?*

The people who had been angry before.

*Did you feed this back to the person who had offended them before?*

Yes. I have lunch with the person from time to time so I can give information without its seeming to come from on high: The white tower has spoken again. One of us in the department will try to develop some sort of informal relationship with the person who has come out of that kind of workshop. For example, over lunch, I might ask, "What are you doing to push forward some of those things we talked about?" We haven't won them all in these cases, but I think we win more than we lose.

*Let me go to step three, the context in which training is done. In many companies people are called in for half a day or two and a half days for what I term skills packages: a bit of this, a bit of that, that are just thrown out there, almost at random. The retention curve is the real enemy, because people get back to the work scene and don't find a good reason to apply the learning or a good way to put it to work. So much of the learning disappears. That's why I've been advocating that management training be presented in a context of motivation. I've developed five practical steps for managers and after I've offered them, then I talk about specific skills and where they can fit in the package. I use Expectancy Theory as the theory base.*

I agree that training should be given in a context of motivation. I haven't called it Expectancy Theory, but I call it the So What Factor. You have to tell employees up front what's expected of them. You have to make sure that the work is seen as more than nickel-and-dime stuff. The work has to be tied to the employee's what's-in-it-for-me. I'm not talking about money. If you don't stick around to watch what they're doing and don't praise them when you get what you want, they'll revert to what they did before. The employees will say, "So what?"

You have to start with the business plan. But then you say to employees, "What would you like your goals to be? What would you like our department to be doing? How can we build in your dreams and aspirations and make you a success along with the department? What would you do if you had a magic wand that allowed you to do what you want that fits within the context of our vision of success?"

*That's pretty enlightened. Lately I've come to the strong suspicion that many managers don't understand the power they have in re-*

*wards. And bringing the employees right into the center of setting goals triggers the motivating forces in them.*

I say to the managers, "When you give them their goals, for whom do employees think they are working and whom do they believe they make look good?" The reality is that employees are going to work hard and productively and efficiently and effectively—all those wonderful words—if they think they are going to be rewarded internally for it and, to some extent, externally. Here's what the employee says: "You'd better tell me when you like what I do, and you don't have to grovel, and you don't have to thank me for coming to work every day, but when I bust my backside for you, I expect you to say you know what I did and that you appreciate it."

In these courses, talking as we do about rewards, we generally have a huge AHA! hit. We use the example of employees coming in late all the time. The manager chastises them for not coming in on time. The next day, when they do arrive on time, the manager sits in the office and says nothing. Well, we tell the managers that when they do that they've lost any motivation that might have been there in the employees. If the managers get up and say to the employees "I'm really glad to see you. Thanks for making the effort," they'll get more on-time behavior. Most of us are like little puppy dogs that go where the petting is.

*You know that I have no problem agreeing with you, but I wonder how you really get this across in training sessions.*

We play the "yeas and boos" game. It's kind of silly, but it works in getting the AHA! We send two people out of the room. Then we decide on three random activities that they will perform once they return. They have to figure it out. The first one we let back into the room, and we only boo when the trainee is doing what we don't want him or her to do. Other than that, we're absolutely silent. Now the next one comes in. We give yeas when they're even close to what we want and we boo when they don't. The light bulbs come on. If I don't give the yeas, I won't get the productivity I want. They see that to get what you want, you have to give both. The boos alone don't usually teach much. Of course, you have the kind of manager who asks, "Why should I reward them for doing what they're paid to do?"

*Oh, yes, that's the military mentality. "That's a clean weapon, soldier." "Thank you, sir." "Don't thank me. That's what you're supposed to have."*

Yes. When the light bulbs start to pop, we ask, "What behavior are you really rewarding?" When you refuse to take corrective action until it's too late and then you hit him with a two by four, what are you saying to the employee? "Don't come to me with your problems; I'll hurt you." We spend a lot of time on this, and we're hearing good things from our managers. Another thing: We don't leave it to them to figure out what they do with this. We do the miniseminars I told you about. They want more.

*Give me an example of a miniseminar that grows out of the overview course.*

Turning around nonperformers, which is corrective counseling. What generally happens in such training courses is "here's a list of how you document, here's a three-tiered step to counseling, and, if you have to terminate, here's how the file looks."

But what we're saying in our miniseminar is, "Hey, people, we have a lot of money invested in this employee. If we really do believe that 99 percent of employees can be turned around—and I do believe that heart and soul—then we need to get behind what we see the employee doing and find out what's going on." Frequently the employee who is a pain is someone who has never found a way to communicate his or her disappointment or frustration, so they nag or whine or whatever. If you act fast enough to get to the real problem, you can generally turn the bad situation around. Our special workshop gets to the heart of not just documentation but how you can rescue the employee.

*"How to deal with the problem employee." I see a lot of seminar announcements with that title. Let me be ironic for a minute, on this subject of deficient performance. Sometimes when I'm speaking*

*to groups of trainers, I'll do a quick and dirty survey. I ask how many of them work for companies with appraisal systems, and most hold up their hands. Then I ask how many of them train the appraisers. Once again, the majority, usually. Finally, I ask, "How many of you work for companies that have appraisal systems that do what they're supposed to do?" This time, only a few hands go up. "What you've just told me," I say, "is that most of you train appraisers to do appraisals that don't work."*

Exactly right. It's a major frustration. We spend a lot of time showing managers that we don't care a hoot and a holler about the form but what we care about is the way we talk to employees and making sure our managers get what they want. This question on performance appraisals is one that all companies struggle with. We've gotten away from a grading system to a sort of pass-fail system. We've broken the direct tie to salary administration, which our managers aren't very happy about because it has made their job much harder. We say, "There's a management activity called performance appraisal and there's a management activity called salary administration, and we're not going to give you a formula as to how to link those two."

*I've always advocated that when you discuss performance you do not discuss the rewards so that the employee will sit there thinking, "What am I going to get?" rather than "What am I supposed to do?"*

Right.

*Now to my next recommendation: Use line managers to deliver training. You do that.*

We do it, but we don't do it as much as we're going to. In the generic programs, that is, the noninsurance programs, we look for opportunities, and we've built in a bunch of them, where we can have a line manager as cofacilitator. There are case studies that they're responsible for developing, and they lead that piece of the seminar.

They have accountability for that part of the program, how it relates and is used back in the department.

We work with them to help them get over the scare factor. But they bring an unbelievable amount of credibility to the course. It doesn't matter what company you're in, if you're from corporate, you're suspect. We're quite open to using line managers, because we have the attitude, and try to convey it, that "we from corporate don't know everything. In fact, you people probably know a lot more than I do. My job is simply to help you to understand how much you really do know." With that attitude, of course you're going to want to use them in the delivery. When they hear us in the course, the anxiety goes down and the receptivity goes up.

Not only do we use line managers in the generic programs but also in sales training. We're building a line of technical training courses that will only be taught by line managers. Our job is to train them how to be facilitators instead of talking heads, and we also make sure that the context of the courses is right. When we're in the room, we're in the back, and the line managers will lead the charge.

*Give me an example of a generic program in which you use line managers.*

Managing client relationships. We don't teach the course unless there's a senior account manager in the room with us sitting at the head of the table. The manager talks about what we've done well at J&H and what we haven't, and what we've learned from that. We give the manager guidance. We might hand him or her half the course: "You handle this section. Here are some things you might want to think about. If you get into trouble, we'll be there to help you."

*In some companies that use line managers, those managers feel there is a stigma attached to training. How do you get around that?*

Training is something we believe in so much that we've built it into our expectations up and down the line. You as a manager may not have a formal assignment of training but you can be assigned as mentor, which is a training role. Somebody else who is very senior will be asked to create an in-house lunch to do a series. Somebody else may be asked to be our contact in the branch office. We try to make sure that training is something that middle and senior people get involved with. We have a philosophy that we have to grow our own, and that's something every person takes seriously.

*How do line managers doing training feel rewarded? You've said this is part of their expectation.*

Part of the reward comes from the limelight we make sure they get. They receive acclamation for the sessions they run. Whenever possible, people who are doing wonderful things are brought before regional or national meetings. When we hear of something good, we make sure our people on the executive floor hear about it, and they'll write notes to the managers acknowledging the good work. Sometimes we publicize accomplishments nationally by sending letters to the branches along with the material that people have developed. "Look what Joe Blow or Susan Smith has put together."

*My fifth recommendation is to provide experiential learning after the classroom. Now we're moving into the real development area.*

This is a fledgling area for us. We're doing some good work here, and there's much more to be done. We start in the classroom. We like to use real-life cases and examples: If we can't tie what we're teaching back to their roles, we have no business teaching it. So we ask them to bring their own world into the course. If we're going to work on a case study, it might as well be a situation they're facing. They may talk about their toughest client, or a negotiation they're in the midst of, or a presentation they have to give next week.

*You really have to get rid of the classroom walls, don't you?*

It's not an easy thing to do, and I don't think we'd be able to do what we do if we didn't make an effort to live in their world. The walls come down more quickly when it becomes obvious to them that we know their language and try to stay abreast of what's happening with them.

*How do you follow up?*

We keep up a pretty good correspondence rate. We ask such things as, "What did you learn?" "What are you using?" "Why aren't you using more?" "Why does it work for you?" As for the trainees' managers, we deal with them in terms of their accountability in demanding a return on their investment.

*How do you do this?*

We send out memos about what's been taught. "Here are the things you need to sit down and talk about with your employees."

*This is part of the original learning contract, isn't it? They have to fulfill it.*

They must fulfill it. We come in later and ask, "What did you do with this stuff? Where's it happening?" We want examples of what works and what doesn't. Again, we've got to work in their world.

*Let's talk some more about managerial accountability. My people have been off on a learning assignment. Now they're back, and I must reinforce the learning. I'm supposed to provide application. To whom am I accountable?*

You are accountable to the manager above you. My accountability is to give your manager as well as you feedback on what people learned. If I see problems developing in your department, for example, that you are not following up, I'll come to you first. If our talk doesn't accomplish anything, I'll go to your manager.

*But you come to me first and have a frank discussion about what I'm not doing that I should be doing. I know what happens if I continue not to do what I'm supposed to do.*

That's right.

*Finally, how do you folks at J&H reward successful learning?*

We reward with money in cases of professional learning that's job related. If you get your master's or a law degree or a CPCU (Chartered Property and Casualty Underwriter), we pay on a graduated scale from $500 to $3,000. As for training, we try to build goals into it and you're accountable for those goals. I haven't been in a meeting in the last three years where we haven't talked to managers about their responsibility to acknowledge it when their subordinates try something new. Just acknowledging it can be a reward.

*When your trainees leave the classroom, they have action plans?*

Yes. And there is accountability, and that's reflected in the performance appraisal. We tell managers also that they should encourage their people who have come back from a course to pass the knowledge on to other people. They are the resident experts. That puts them in the limelight, which can be a reward. And here at PD, we bestow rewards. Some of the people who do well in certain courses, say writing skills, are asked whether they'd like to teach them. We'll train them to be the resident experts and trainers in their branches.

There's one other benefit that comes from in-house training that I'm not sure many trainers quite appreciate: We can help our trainees to create their own liaisons in the company. After all, you're coming to a course with people from a variety of branches and departments.

*What kind of response are you getting from managers on this reward issue?*

I think for the first couple of years they had to get used to funny language like reward systems, but now they're trying to reward their people and they see it works. There have been a lot of success stories about correcting and improving performance.

*I'm a creature of corporate life, about thirty years. I've always heard managers talk about rewards, but I think many of them don't really understand that they have such power to influence behavior through rewards. Do you share that suspicion?*

I do.

*They haven't made the link.*

We're beginning to here. Part of the problem is that Americans tend to think simplistically about this area of management. A reward to them is money, and when they're dealing with tight salary budgets, as everyone is, they say they don't have any way to give rewards.

*Well, as you say, just acknowledging new behavior is a reward. I tell managers they have an infinite supply of praise. It's cheap. And it works.*

# ■ 10 ■

# Developing Better
# Influencing and Negotiating Skills

Successful salespeople are the most skilled people in dealing with others that I have ever seen. The sales professionals who know what they are doing are trained in skills that most nonselling managers would pay a lot of money to acquire—if they really understood influencing skills. And since many sales transactions are negotiations, inside managers can benefit enormously.

It's a link that has escaped many people, trainers and managers, probably because they haven't been trained, as I have, in basic selling techniques. Most managers, I suspect, are not ready to be told that not only should they learn sales skills but that they are already selling, whether they know it or not. My recent experience with nonsales people in speeches, seminars, and workshops leads me to believe that they still are not prepared to understand the value of being salespeople.

Managers have ideas, projects, priorities, and goals that they hope higher management will accept. They even suggest that their bosses consider them for advancement or more responsibility. Obviously, salespeople have their products, programs, concepts, and services to sell. A manager with a keen sense of the political will try to understand what the decision makers see as valuable to them, what they would find attractive in an idea or proposal. Managers who are influencers study the people who can say yes. Salespeople understand that they must know their prospects' needs and wants. Persuasive managers know that they are well advised to present solutions to problems and needs if they are to win the attention of higher management. Salespeople involve their prospects in the sales transaction, showing the prospects how what the salespeople have to offer will meet those needs and wants. Clearly, what salespeople do is much the same as what managers do. They try to persuade others to accept what they propose.

### Five Persuasive Steps in Selling

Managers often meet resistance to their ideas. Salespeople do too, but the difference is that salespeople expect to have to deal with opposition and they are trained to do so. Managers are often surprised, are not usually trained to handle resistance, and often don't know what to do when they encounter opposition or disagreement. Yet the same techniques that salespeople use to disarm a resistant prospect work admirably well between managers and those whom they are trying to convince—against odds.

Let's look at the five steps in the persuasive process that we train salespeople in and see how they fit supposedly nonsales transactions.

1.   Know your product.
2.   Know your prospect.
3.   Involve your prospect.
4.   Ask for the action you want.
5.   Be prepared to handle opposition.

*The Universality of Selling.* The five steps above cover virtually any kind of transaction in which someone wants something from someone else—approval, cooperation, acceptance. A safety engineer suggests a new type of valve for his company's storage tanks. A chemist argues for a new solvent to be used in a manufacturing process. A director of human resources proposes that her corporation set up a pilot quality circles program. A line manager appeals to his subordinates to put forth extra effort during a period of emergency. The five steps can be useful in adversarial situations in which the two sides have a conflict to resolve. Skillful and open use of persuasive techniques can bring the parties closer together.

The advantages of training managers in selling skills may be obvious, but when you introduce such training, you'd better be prepared to handle immediate resistance. Usually initial opposition on the part of trainees is to the notion that they are selling. Some trainers therefore try to disguise the process by using nonsales language. For example, "Know what you want accepted or implemented." Or "What are the interests and needs of the decision makers?" Some of the language can get pretty lofty and psychological.

My approach has been to keep the training simple and straightforward. Thus, I keep the sales terms in the design. However, I ease into the presentation by spending much time talking about the various kinds of transactions that the average person enters into in organizational life. I encourage the trainees to describe their experiences in trying to influence others, both successful and unsuccessful. I frequently emphasize that the successful transactions, both in the short term and long, are those that are open and nonmanipulative. The initial obstacle that I work to overcome is that many people have stereotyped salespeople as cunning and underhanded and even as con people. By continuing to insist on the openness of transactions and on the rewards of following the five persuasive steps, you can hope to overcome the squeamishness of trainees toward the selling process.

The next barrier you encounter in trainees will probably be in steps 2—know your prospect—and 3—involve your prospect. Many of the problems in communicating and resolving conflicts in organizations stem from the conviction in people involved that their perception of the situation or their solution to the problem or the decision they have suggested is the only correct one. "It makes sense to me; therefore, it should make sense to you as well." "This is the way it is; why are you too stubborn to accept it?" In one high-tech company, staff specialists made recommendations to the plant or production for new equipment or techniques. If the manager hesitated to accept the recommendation or questioned its wisdom, it was not uncommon for the specialist to throw up his hands and walk away, saying, "The hell with it." It's not surprising that man-

agement called me in to help these folks become a bit more understanding and patient in their communicating.

I tend to believe that interpersonal failures very often orig-
inate in people's lack of empathy for and acceptance of the perceptions and positions of others. Additionally, you'll often find that
people believe that logic is all that matters. "If I believe I have logic
on my side, you have no options left other than caving in to me."
The experienced salesperson understands well that most transactions take place on both a rational and a nonrational level. People
have rational objectives, and they have emotional or psychological
objectives.

*Recognizing Needs and Wants.* The initial steps in training managers to use selling techniques should involve their understanding
and recognizing the rational and nonrational, the tangible and intangible aspects of transactions. It's probably true that all successful
persuading involves the intangible and nonrational. (Incidentally,
it is important at the outset to make a clear distinction between
*non*rational and *ir*rational. Many people confuse the two.) I'll illustrate with a problem that arose in a group of insurance loss control
specialists who regularly examine the facilities of policyholders to
recommend ways they can make their properties safer and cut the
risks of injury and liability. One participant cited the instance of
a storage tank with a valve that the engineer considered potentially
dangerous. When he recommended that the executive in charge substitute a different and admittedly somewhat better valve to ensure
greater safety, the man objected. "That valve has functioned well for
years," he said. "I don't see any reason to replace it." The loss
control representative tossed the objection to me. "What can you
do," he asked, "when the policyholder makes a statement of truth
like that?"

My response to that kind of common question is another
question: "What are you really selling?" The engineer believes he
is selling a valve, but that's a small part of the transaction. Most
sales involve intangibles—in this case, peace of mind. Here's how
the engineer would frame his product: "Mr. X, from looking
around your plant and talking with your people, I know you have
a high concern for their well-being. It's true that there is a possi-

bility that the older valve will continue to function, and there is also a possibility—maybe slight—that suddenly it will give way or leak. If that happens, and if even one employee is placed at risk or injured, I know that you would be terribly distressed at seeing one of your people carried out of here on a stretcher. I recommend the new valve, because I'm sure that, once it is in, you'll sleep better." How much is peace of mind worth?

If I ask trainers to tell me what their product is, I invariably get the response, "Training programs." Nonsense. Trainers are selling improved performance that affects the bottom line.

In some of my workshops, I gave the management trainees an exercise in which they were to imagine that they had been asked to form a task force to study flextime and to make recommendations for its adoption by their company. The manager in the exercise had to recruit his or her task force members from colleagues' departments. One other manager, a woman who was considered a fast-tracker and who enjoyed semiautonomy because of higher management's respect for her, held out. She wasn't sure she could spare the specialist the task force organizer wanted. My question was, "How can you persuade her to say yes?"

The responses were quite predictable. Some trainees would have lectured her on the benefits of flextime to the company. In other words, they would have run the flag up and suggested that she salute it. Others would have hinted at punishment: You wouldn't want me to have to say to higher management that you wouldn't cooperate. Still another appeal to her patriotism was the implied accusation that by withholding her employee when others had cooperated, she would not be considered a team player. All of these are variations on the theme: This is the correct thing to do, and you had better do it.

Every so often, one bright and creative management trainee would ask himself or herself, "How could what I propose be beneficial to her?" One answer is that this woman obviously, from the exercise description, liked control. A selling point, therefore, might be, "This task force will make decisions and suggestions that might affect your operation. I'm sure you'd want to be in on that decision-making process."

Each workshop simply reinforced my belief that many people in responsible positions in corporations are not conditioned to think about other people's needs and wants. It doesn't take much imagination to envision how much easier it would be to get cooperation from others, to negotiate mutually acceptable decisions, to get approval for projects, to resolve disagreements if the people affected involved the others by showing how the others would benefit by extending cooperation: to join in a good decision, to approve the project, or to put conflict to rest. What are some of the benefits? A better image, more glory, more prestige and status, or a relatively trouble-free relationship. And let's not forget the benefit that is too seldom talked about these days in our serious world: having more fun doing our jobs.

### Getting to Yes

From my experience, I would assume that asking for the order, or for the action desired, is about as difficult on the inside as it is in the sales prospect's office. People are hesitant to ask directly for what they want, and when they don't ask, and don't get it, they can become awfully frustrated. In one company, the top management group met every other week. One of the vice-presidents, a very intelligent man, frequently wrote long, analytical, and sometimes brilliant memos to his colleagues in the management group. But to his astonishment, and eventually to his disgust, none of his colleagues brought up the memos in the biweekly groups. His behavior in the meetings changed; he became abrasive and tactless. No one doubted the value of his contributions, but they were simply unpleasant to hear after a time.

A consultant was brought in to help the management group plan and do a little team building. Almost immediately, the consultant sensed the enormous hostility of the vice-president toward his colleagues. Hearing about the memos, the consultant asked to read them—and found a clue to the anger. Nowhere in the memos did the vice-president ask his colleagues to discuss them at the regular meetings: They waited for him to bring them up; he expected them to do so. In the spirit of good selling, the consultant advised the vice-president to tell the group what he wanted from them. A simple request to put the item on the agenda sufficed from then on.

A decided benefit in training managers to sell is that much of the mystery and hard work go out of communicating. Many people belong to what I call the Agatha Christie school of communicating: See if you can figure out what I want from you. Since most people are disinclined to work any harder than they must, they may become quite annoyed with having to do the work to understand what the other person is trying to say. And the person trying to communicate is building suspense because he or she is under the illusion that a good case must be built to support the request. Unfortunately, by the time the requester gets around to asking for the action he or she wants, the other person has tuned out. After sales training, managers are more likely to make it clear up front what they want and then explain why it is a good idea.

There are a number of ways to "close," as a salesperson would say. You can emphasize the major benefit of the proposal and ask for approval or acceptance. You can summarize all the benefits you've been describing and lead right into the request for action. You can use what we call the penalty/reassurance close: Here's what we stand to lose if we don't take this action now. Those are just a few of the ways people can lead from the presentation right into the request to buy.

### Handling Resistance

Salespeople understand that when they introduce a new idea, product, way of thinking, or change, there will probably be at least some initial opposition to the prospect. Managers experience the same phenomenon. They suggest a change, and immediately someone comes up with a reason not to accept it. In sales parlance we call them objections: There's no money in the budget; higher management would never go for that; we tried it once and it didn't work; we are so pressed for time now that we couldn't fit this in. Or they are stalls: This is really not the best time; why don't we table this until next year; first we have to do such-and-such and then we can consider this. They're reasons not to buy, or not to buy now.

Salespeople are usually trained to deal with opposition. Managers, who encounter resistance frequently from bosses or other managers or subordinates, are usually not trained accordingly. Consequently, many people get defensive or angry, or feel threatened, or lose control of the situation and ramble and argue. Generally such behaviors aren't helpful in advancing the cause of a good idea or project or of cooperation and commitment.

I advocate that managers be trained in a six-step technique for handling the resistance that is usually bound to come with any suggestion of change:

1. Relax
2. Listen
3. Accept
4. Move on
5. Qualify the objection and answer it briefly
6. Ask for action

Most people who feel challenged or disagreed with react fairly quickly. They want to rebut the opposition or even to undermine the credibility or authority of the person offering the objection. It's a natural reaction. The proposer believes that the person who offers opposition probably doesn't quite understand the idea or doesn't have all the facts, so there's a rush to supply the missing information. It's an assumption that may not be true.

When I train salespeople (as well as managers), I caution them against jumping in quickly to answer an objection or to overcome a stall. Interestingly, I often get resistance at this point. Why not take care of the resistance immediately, I'm asked? There are a number of reasons. First, you've been positive in describing your idea: Why turn negative? Stay positive. Second, if you respond right away, you may unwittingly reinforce the objection. He or she might not have considered it a weighty issue until you treated it as such, but the person offering it suddenly realizes how seriously you take it. The most important reason, however, is that the objection may not be real.

When people aren't sold or convinced, they often throw up some sort of barrier that's easy to construct and likely to avoid an argument. For example, you've been approached by an employee of another department who would like to transfer into your operation. You petition your boss for permission to accept her. He says, "We really aren't budgeted for another person." That's an objection. Is it real? You don't know. It's easy for the boss to put you off with the budget argument. Or he may say, "Well, her boss is having a little problem, and if we took her away at this moment, it would complicate things for that department." That's a stall. Is it real? You don't know. What the boss may be hoping is that you accept the objection or the stall and walk away without any argument. The truth could very well be that he just doesn't want to make the decision at this time. You can argue all you want against either objection, but if they're not real, you're wasting your time and risking annoying the boss.

*Relax and Listen.* Let me provide an example from my own experience. A few years ago, over lunch, I was "pitching" a new book idea to a publisher who had already issued three of my books, all of which were either profitable or on their way to being money-makers. The book was to be a manual of participative techniques for the manager who wanted a more open and democratic work group. It was an idea, incidentally, that the publisher himself had mentioned some months earlier, and consequently, I expected an easy sale. But now he looked doubtful. "I don't know," he said. "Maybe if you gave me an outline and a couple of chapters . . ."

At that point I had at least three major options. I could agree to his suggestion, but I didn't understand where his resistance was coming from, so I wasn't sure that supplying the outline and the sample chapters would have satisfied him. I really suspected he was putting me off, hoping that he wouldn't have to make the decision for a while, if ever. My second course of action was to refuse to do what he asked; I generally don't like to supply sample chapters out of context. But I sensed that my refusal would have ended the discussion. After all, he didn't have to publish the book, and why should he feel an obligation if he wasn't sold?

I chose the third option. "Sure," I said, "no problem." Then I went on talking about how I saw the book. Again, he asked for the outline and the chapters. And again I said, "Sure." I talked further about the book. He began to look more interested. I paused to let him think. After a moment, he smiled and said, abruptly, "Let's do it." We did, and interestingly, that book, *Inspiring People at Work: How to Make Participative Management Work for You* (1986) became one of my best sellers. I have never believed that choosing the other two options would have gotten me anywhere.

Often the best way to handle resistance is not to handle it— or at least not to seem to handle it. I tell managers to relax when they meet opposition or disagreement. That's probably far from what many do when they fear that their ideas are being discounted or discarded. They are usually tempted to pour on more pressure, or they resort to the old school of selling that I label the wear-'em-down approach: If they don't buy at first, keep repeating why they should until they can't take it anymore. In sales, you can still see vestiges of the wear-'em-down school, but not often. Inside, however, in corporate offices and conference rooms, the school's traditions are widely honored.

Relax, I say. Sit back. Cross your legs. Look mildly interested but not puzzled or fearful. Your relaxation will usually disarm your critic, who expects you to fight. Now, by not talking, by looking interested, you signal that you are prepared to listen. Don't smile. That could be construed as condescending. You want the other person to tell you what's on his or her mind. If you don't hear it, you don't know what you're up against. You may discover that the person hasn't understood you or has some simple-minded notions that you can easily destroy. Resist the temptation to rebut. The more your critic talks, the more ammunition you have to fire back later.

*Accept but Don't Agree.* As you read this, I hope you are envisioning quieter conversations, more peaceful and constructive meetings, fewer red faces, less noise pollution, and vastly reduced wheel-spinning.

The next step seems, for many managers, to go against the grain of traditional behavior. Accept what the other person is saying, no matter now bewildered you are that he or she could take seriously what is being said. I suggest that one of the greatest impediments to communicating, to understanding, to persuading is the failure of managers to do something that is very simple: Accept the reality that the other person thinks or feels the way he or she expresses. Acceptance is not agreement. By accepting the other person's thoughts and words and feelings, you honor him or her, who at this point is probably not expecting to be so honored. "Yes," you might say, "I see that you feel that way," or "I can see that that is important to you," or "I accept that that is a consideration with you."

Success in solving problems, in managing conflict, and in closing gaps in understanding often hinges on this very simple act: accepting others. I remember someone's criticism of Walter Cronkite's words that closed out his nightly news program: "And that's the way it was . . ." The critic said that the fact that Walter Cronkite saw it that way was not necessarily evidence that it really was that way: It was the newscaster's perception. It's a good point, because many of us start negotiating not by giving our version of the problem or situation but by "telling it like it is." When we broadcast to others that our perceptions are the correct ones, we wonder why we don't get any further.

One indisputable benefit of training your managers in sales skills is that they begin to understand much more clearly how essential it is to assume that the other person has interests, needs, and perceptions that might be different from theirs. Furthermore, they understand that the other person believes his or her interests, needs, and perceptions are just as valid as anyone else's. Accepting this reality doesn't guarantee success in communicating and negotiating, but it's doubtful that success can be achieved without it.

*Move On: Sidestep and Sell.* We can accomplish a whole revolution in communicating and negotiating if we banish forever the phrase "Yes, but . . ." Substitute "Yes, and . . ." and amazing things happen. Here's what often occurs when a person meets resistance:

*Boss:*   Henry, it's a good idea, but I think it's just too elaborate for us.

*Henry:*   Yes, but it's working very well in Jerrold's department, and I've got an adaptation here that will work for us.

And here's another example:

*Boss:*   Your proposal is interesting, but I don't think it will be cost-effective, John.

*John:*　Yes, but it only looks as if it would be expensive. When you study the savings in the first six months, you'll find . . .

And here's the prizewinner:

*Colleague:*　Emily, I know I can speak for all of us here that you have turned in a most impressive proposal. It's evident that you have put in so much time and the quality of work that we have come to expect from you permeates every page. I think you should be very proud of yourself. However, on balance, there do seem to be some compelling arguments to take a further look at the implications of your suggestions just to make sure that we can do justice to your creative thinking, and therefore, as much as I regret having to say this, we have to postpone final consideration of this until after the first of the year . . . blah, blah, blah . . . and blah.

*Emily:*　Yes, but if we don't move on this now, we could lose out on a marvelous opportunity to save money.

These people are all yes-butting each other. Their responses, however seemingly tactfully phrased, come down to such unkindnesses as "I know you think you know what you're talking about, but you don't." Or, "I don't care what you say; you're wrong." They are all unncesssary irritants and putdowns.

It is so easy to say instead, "Yes, I see that you think that way, and here's something else you might want to mull over." Or, "While you're considering, here's something else you'll want to consider." Move on to give them another reason why they should approve your suggestion or proposal. "Yes, and . . ." messages accept. "Yes, but . . ." messages deny.

Denial is frequent in managerial communications. To a colleague who expresses concern about a proposal the manager has put forth, the manager responds, "Don't worry. There's no problem there." It's not a soothing message. The translation is "You don't know what you're talking about." To the employee who complains that the manager has given her an unfair evaluation, the manager says, "I won't listen to that. I may be tough on you, but I'm fair." This is denial: "You have no right to your feelings." In sales training, we learn that other people believe they do have a right to their feelings and we hurt our influence with them when we deny that right.

When you accept the other person's beliefs or feelings and gracefully step aside to supply more reasons why the person should say yes to you, you avoid discounting or putting down that person. Eventually, as you gently persist, you will probably find out whether the initial objection was real. If the other person continues to say, "I still feel it costs too much," then you know you truly have what the salesperson would call a price objection. On the other hand, you may suddenly hear something quite different: "What you're asking me to do negates what I have been doing all these years, and everything in me says no." Now you have the truth. Had you spent your time arguing about price, you would have trained your artillery on ground fog.

In training managers to sell, I like to do role plays at this point. I do not tell them in advance about the six steps. I simply say, "My associate and I are going to simulate a sales situation. I will be the person trying to persuade her, and she will be my prospect. Listen carefully to everything we say, and watch what we do. Later, I'll ask you for your analysis." During the role play, I relax. I obviously listen, because I sometimes repeat what my associate has said to me. I accept. I move on to sell more reasons.

When I ask the observers what has happened, I find they have missed even the obvious behavior and words. I have long been aware that most people do not listen well without training, but these role plays have taught me that people are also not skillful observers without training. The salesperson is taught to process what goes on during the transaction, but most other people don't know how. They must be trained to observe and analyze the significance of what they see and hear.

Lately I've read articles and heard of research that show that many executives at the top issue policies and directives, blithely ignorant that such words from on high do not reach the lower levels, or are not understood at those levels in the way the issuing executives intend. The difficulty that many trainees show in my workshops in hearing, seeing, and analyzing leads me to suggest that no manager, no matter how close he or she may be to subordinates, can safely assume that his or her words and actions are automatically understood by employees. You can only be sure that they know what you intend them to know if there is feedback. You must find ways of asking your subordinates, "What did you hear? What is your understanding?" When you hear your meanings coming back at you, then you can relax.

*Qualify Objections and Ask for Action.* Finally, when you realize that you have a genuine objection or the real reason for the stall, you can reach step 5: Qualify the objection. It's a very simple technique: If I can show you how we accomplish this without busting the budget (or without causing disruption, or by actually increasing the prestige of our department), would you be favorable to moving ahead with it?" If the resistance is out in the open, the answer is usually yes. Your next step is to provide your solution, to answer the objection, to ease your way around the stall.

Then you follow up with step 6: Ask for action. "Will you OK this?" "May I have your go-ahead?" "Will you approve this?" Often the answer is positive. But if you get a no, you can feel free to say, "What has to happen for us to move ahead on this?"

### Polishing Influencing and Negotiating Skills

Sales training for managers raises their awareness in a number of areas:

- Other people have needs and interests that are as valid for them as yours are for you.
- If you are to get their acceptance of your ideas and proposals, you must be prepared to show them that what you offer will meet their needs and wants.
- Most people enter into transactions willingly if they see the possibility that they will gain something valuable.
- Resistance is a natural part of problem solving, decision making, and any form of persuading and can usually be dealt with successfully with patience, acceptance, and understanding.
- Most people make decisions on rational and nonrational levels. When you try to persuade people to accept you and your ideas,

remember not only to provide them with logic but with emotional and psychological gratification as well. You are, in most cases, selling intangibles.

An effective sales training program can take two or three days. Trainees can adopt the concepts and practice techniques in that time.

In my research on influential people over the past two decades, I've identified eight characteristics that many of them share:

1. *Influential people know what they want.* They are very goal-oriented, and they are very clear about their goals.
2. *Influential people have a right to try to get what they want.* They may not get what they want, but nothing shakes their confidence in going after it.
3. *Influential people are articulate.* They make sure that other people understand what they want to communicate.
4. *Influential people are sensitive.* They understand how important it is to understand the needs and wants of those whom they wish to influence—bosses, colleagues, subordinates.
5. *Influential people have credibility.* They recognize that this is essential to persuading others, and they take care not to put it at risk.
6. *Influential people know how to deal with opposition.* They appreciate how important it is to stay in control of the persuasive process.
7. *Influential people know how to ask for the action they want.* When you deal with them, you always know what they want from you.
8. *Influential people know what motivates others.* They know the value of rewards in influencing people to accept what they offer.

If these characteristics describe the kind of people you want working for you and your organization, know that you can train your subordinates to be influential people.

# ■ 11 ■

# Using Assertiveness Training to Improve Communication

My surveys tell me that relatively few people in organizations today have been through assertiveness training. That's a pity, because assertiveness can be useful in helping a person not only to identify his or her needs but also to express them in a manner that is acceptable to other people. By using assertiveness techniques, we can often say unpleasant things that people really don't want to hear and succeed in getting their attention.

Unfortunately, assertiveness training doesn't seem to be as popular as it was a decade ago, when many women who were entering the work force found it helpful in learning to hold their own in a male-dominated business world. This kind of training apparently became so closely tied to the rise in feminism that it didn't catch on much with men. At least, that's my impression.

In recent years, I've been urging the training community to take a closer look at the value of assertiveness training, and I have heartily recommended it for managers. The primary virtue of assertiveness training is that it provides a simple formula for communicating one's perceptions, feelings, and needs to others. When the formula is followed, the result is greater clarity and more authenticity than we find in much communicating between people in organizations. As a listener, when the other person is employing

161

assertiveness techniques, you don't have to wonder about what the other person is getting at or feeling or what he or she wants from you. It's all up front.

When you put managers through assertiveness training, you give them the skills to help them avoid some of the demotivating behaviors that managers often exhibit when they communicate with their subordinates. At one end of the managerial behavior range, for example, is aggressiveness, which is characterized by words and manner of speaking that humiliate, embarrass, belittle. Here's a manager bawling out an employee who has made certain repeated mistakes: "How many times have I told you this is not the way I want it done? Whether you realize it or not, I have good reasons for wanting it done my way. But you continue to ignore me. I don't know whether it's because you don't listen to me, or whether you just can't get it through your head what I'm telling you."

It's not unlikely that you've heard that kind of feedback directed at some hapless individual from a manager. The manager suggests that the employee is deficient, either in listening skills or in intelligence. True, managers get exasperated, lose patience, become angry at times, but feedback given this way usually invites resentment and sullenness rather than correction and improvement. Yet in many profiles of managers in the business press, we read that they are hard-driving, demanding, and often abrasive in their styles of communicating with the people who report to them.

It's fine to be demanding. No one questions a manager's right to be hard-driving, pushy, ambitious, but aggressive behavior is *never* justified in a manager—or in anyone else, for that matter. Leona Helmsley in a CBS "60 Minutes" broadcast described herself as "tough but fair." Tough, yes, but watching the footage of her dealing with her hotel employees, I couldn't say that I regarded her as fair. Her criticisms of employees were horrifying. The purpose of feedback, or communicating in general, is to get some kind of correction or other result. It should never be used to destroy someone.

### The Unsuitability of Nonassertiveness

If aggressive behavior means rolling over others, nonassertiveness, the other extreme on the scale, means permitting yourself to be rolled over by others. It is no more acceptable in a manager than aggressiveness. The aggressive manager conveys the clear message that he or she doesn't like your behavior and is not terribly fond of you, either. Such a manager says, in Transactional Analysis terms, "I'm OK, but you definitely are not OK." The nonassertive manager seems to suggest that he or she is not OK. Here's an example of a manager who takes his subordinate to task for some long lunch hours: "Marty, got a minute? Come on into the office, and let's chat. I really haven't had much of a chance to just relax with you lately. Well, you know how it is. The squeaky wheels and all that. If I had a whole department of people like you I wouldn't have much to do. All the time you've been with me—what is it, eight years?—you've always been so conscientious. I never had to worry much about your reliability. Speaking of that, I thought I'd mention the fact that lately you've been taking rather long lunch hours. It's no big deal. In fact, if it were up to me, I couldn't care less. But the boss said something about it the other day. So I guess I'd better be a good manager and just say a word. Don't worry, but if you can trim a little of the time off the lunch time, it would look better, I suppose. Some people get uptight about these things. But you and I never had to spend much time thinking about appearances. Not when the substance is so real. After all, you've always been one of the most productive people I know . . ."

You probably realize that this manager has used the old sandwich technique on poor Marty: a slab of criticism between two thin slices of praise. It's a mixed message, which is quite common for nonassertive managers. Note also that the boss blames the need for the feedback on his boss—he won't take responsibility at all.

As Marty walks out of the office, he will probably feel uncomfortable. He's really not quite sure what has happened. True, he heard some good things about himself, but in the middle of it all, he was mildly criticized for taking excessive time off for lunch. After reflection, Marty will believe that he has been manipulated. Indeed he has. He got a mixed message designed to disarm him and keep him from being upset or defensive. The criticism contaminated the praise, and the praise diluted the criticism. His manager couldn't tolerate the idea of seeming to come down on Marty, so he disguised the feedback as much as he could.

Nonassertive managers play games. If there is any way they can find to perform their managerial functions without being direct or exposing themselves to negative emotions in subordinates, they will find it. In my career, I have worked for two nonassertive managers, and I found that I could not trust either one to be open or honest with me. I also discovered that both managers would sacrifice me in a minute if they thought it would protect them from unpleasantness, such as criticism from above for any action of mine. The nonassertive manager frequently looks for people he or she can toss from the lifeboat to enhance the survival of the rest (chiefly him- or herself).

### Assertiveness

Assuming that the situation as you see it or experience it at the moment is not what you want, you have to ask yourself in assertiveness training, "What is my perception of what is going on?" "What is a preferable option?" Here are the four steps in communicating assertively:

1.   Describe the situation, what you see going on.
2.   Describe how you feel about what is going on.
3.   Decide what change you'd like.
4.   Decide on the reward to the other in making the change.

You can see how in following the assertive techniques you are forced to focus on change and the future—not the focus of a lot of conflict resolution and problem solving, which often is a CYA activity, a whodunnit. Many times people in organizations worry about where the blame may be placed. Recalling the childhood party game, one sits there wondering whose donkey the tail will be pinned on.

Robert Morton, a psychologist with whom I was associated for a time, always impressed me with his insistence, in the problem-solving and team-building groups he worked with, that people look for alternatives rather than fix blame. In his view, if you had a conflict or an interpersonal or intergroup problem, you should ask yourself this question: "Assuming we don't like what is going on now, what would be a more desirable alternative?" It's a much more productive direction than finding out who did what to whom and when. A few years ago, I sat with a management group as a facilitator and listened as they opened up and tried to settle some old scores with the president, whom they blamed for a series of poor decisions. In the midst of the heat and frenzy, one manager suggested that they stop worrying about what was wrong and who was to blame for it and concentrate instead on how to take care of the problems. Despite my reinforcing the comment, however, the frenzy and finger-pointing continued.

Assertive techniques help people avoid that kind of destructive session. In the training, I insist that people stick to describing behavior when they talk about what they see going on—stay away from suppositions, attitudes, motives, possible psychological causes, and simply describe the behavior they see. For example, you are sitting in a meeting in which one of your colleagues constantly interrupts your comments. You could tell her that you believe she is undisciplined, doesn't respect your contributions, is rude and boorish, all of which will probably gain you a big fight. Instead, talk about her behavior. "There have been several times during this meeting when you broke in on what I was saying and started to talk about something else. I'm very frustrated because I haven't been able to make my points. I would like you to stay quiet until I have finished saying what I want to say. I don't think you want to make me so angry that I can't work with you, and I believe you want this meeting to be productive, which it won't be if you keep cutting me off and making me mad."

That's a good assertive statement. This is what I see. This is what I feel about it. This is what I'd like you to do instead. And this will be the reward to you and all of us if you make the change.

## Responsiveness

Assertiveness is not, strictly speaking, midway on the scale of behavior between aggressiveness and responsiveness. Its placement is nearer aggressiveness than nonassertiveness. When you are assertive, you are primarily concerned with you, secondarily concerned with the other.

| Aggressiveness | Assertiveness | Nonassertiveness |
|---|---|---|
| Totally you, excluding others | Primarily you, secondarily others | Totally others, excluding you |

Assertive behavior is bound to improve much communicating. But being asssertive doesn't always encourage a dialogue or, as I put it in the preceding section, a transaction in which both people want to emerge from something that is valuable to them.

Consultant Malcolm Shaw, who has done much work in this area for the American Management Association, has complemented assertiveness with responsiveness. Assertiveness is a talking mode; responsiveness is more a listening posture. As I made very clear in the preceding section, in a transaction involving two people, there are probably two sets of needs and wants. When you add the responsive mode to assertiveness, you create the environment for negotiation. Here's the scale of behavior with responsiveness added:

| Aggressiveness | Assertiveness | Responsiveness | Nonassertiveness |
|---|---|---|---|
| Totally you, excluding others | Primarily you, secondarily others | Primarily others, secondarily you | Totally others, excluding you |

Following is a comparison between the two modes:

| *Assertiveness* | *Responsiveness* |
|---|---|
| Gives information | Seeks information |
| Expresses feelings | Accepts the feelings of the other without necessarily agreeing with them |
| Describes behavior change desired in others | Seeks a change of behavior in self |
| Sells benefits of change to others | Sells self on benefits of change |

***Choosing Responsiveness.*** There are certainly appropriate times for you as a manager to place yourself in a responsive mode, and some of these are in the following situations:

- You take over an operation that is new to you; you want to learn about the way things are done, the culture of the organization, and how employees feel about the work and the organization.
- You set goals and want people to express to you what aspects of the work and what potential accomplishments are important to them.
- You are counseling an employee on a work-related problem or a performance deficiency, and you are not quite sure what might be causing the problem. You have to draw the employee out to find out how he or she views the situation and to get agreement that a problem exists.
- An employee has suffered a personal loss or is enduring a crisis in his or her personal life.
- You are confronted by an employee who is in an intensely emotional state, and you may feel that for the moment it would not help to counter aggression or assertion with your own assertiveness.
- You are at a meeting and you want to encourage others to assume leadership positions in the group without being intimidated by your presence or your opinions.
- You are listening to an employee for whom you have the greatest admiration or respect.

In general, you want to be responsive in any kind of interaction in which you suspect that the other person brings knowledge or resources to the discussion that could be useful. And whether a lot of managers realize it or not—and I suspect they do not—that covers most substantive discussions with any co-worker.

*The Importance of Flexibility.* In many discussions and interviews, managers will probably move back and forth between assertiveness and responsiveness. The assertive-responsive approach has the following characteristics:

- It acknowledges the rights and feelings of each person in the transaction.
- It creates a dialogue in which each person feels comfortable expressing feelings about what is going on.

- It recognizes that each person has needs, wants, and resources. The resolution or outcome may be, but need not be, all one person's effort.

Following is a brief discussion between a manager and her subordinate, Marla. It illustrates how a sensitive manager can move between assertiveness and responsiveness.

*Manager:*    Marla, your evaluation of the work-flow experiment was due three days ago. I've seen nothing from you. Am I correct that we agreed on last Monday as the deadline?

*Marla:*    Yes, we did. But I'm still working on it.

*Manager:*    Well, that upsets me. An agreement is an agreement. And I'm embarrassed because my boss expected to hear from me. Knowing you, I can't believe you're happy about it.

*Marla:*    I'm very upset.

*Manager:*    There's a simple solution. When you agree with me on a deadline, do your best to meet it. That way, we'll both be happy, and we'll certainly work together more comfortably.

Note that the manager asserted herself—describing the situation and her feelings, spelling out the change of behavior she wants and the reward to Marla for making it. At the same time, the manager was responsive, checking with her subordinate to make sure that both have the same understanding of the situation. She also suspects that Marla, being a conscientious worker, is disappointed over not meeting the deadline.

*Marla:*    It isn't that simple. We agreed on last Monday as a deadline only because you offered to let Ted work with me. After all, Ted knows more about the planning of the experiment than anyone else. But for the past two weeks, Ted tells me that you have had him working on a rush project. He said he couldn't give me any time. So I went it alone.

*Manager:*    Yes, I did ask Ted to rush that through for me. It didn't occur to me at the time that it would inconvenience you. I guess next time when I offer someone else's services to you I'd better check with you before I make another assignment.

*Marla:*   It would help you to get your report on time.

The manager learned something that will be quite useful to her in the future, because she was open and responsive to the feedback that Marla provided her.

### Profile of the Assertive-Responsive Manager

I freely and fearlessly predict that any manager who practices assertive-responsive techniques in communicating with co-workers will begin to enjoy the following benefits:

- It's easy to initiate discussions and to offer feedback to the assertive-responsive (A-R) manager.
- People generally feel comfortable telling the A-R manager what they believe he or she ought to know rather than what the manager would like to hear.
- The A-R manager believes that he or she has the right to make his or her wishes, needs, wants, and expectations known to co-workers, just as they have an equal right to communicate theirs to him or her.
- Others are confident that when the A-R manager feels angry, frustrated, or distressed, he or she will express those feelings in an honest, open manner.
- When the A-R manager does not like the conditions under which he or she and others must work, the manager takes steps to change them or to persuade others to change them.
- When the A-R manager has a problem to work out with another, he or she will allow ample time for the other person to express his or her feelings, will actually encourage that person to do so, even when the person seems hostile.
- The A-R manager is accustomed to showing that he or she believes and trusts co-workers as well as having them show that they trust him or her.
- When the A-R manager is in conflict with others, his or her

tendency is to deal with the issues of the conflict rather than the personalities of the disputants.

- The A-R manager regards himself or herself as an expert on his or her perceptions and feelings and looks at others as being expert about theirs.
- He or she enjoys respectful relationships with others, regardless of whether they all like one another.
- When criticized, the A-R manager seriously considers the content of the negative feedback before responding.
- You generally know what the A-R manager wants or expects of you.

The manager who can be both assertive and responsive is usually more effective with employees today than the manager who is predominantly assertive, because the members of the contemporary work force expect to be respected, esteemed, listened to, and recognized as having ideas and knowledge about the work they do. They bring talents, strengths, and resources to their jobs and to their communications with their managers. Perhaps most important, they have personal goals that they hope to achieve through helping their managers achieve theirs and those of the organization. Often their bosses find that through being responsive as well as assertive they are able to remove obstacles to good performance and goals achievement that prevent the employees from being satisfied in the work.

An excellent source for you to plan training for your subordinates in assertive-responsive behavior is *Assertive-Responsive Management,* by Malcolm Shaw (1979). An alternative is my book, *Managing for Peak Performance* (1989a).

# ■ 12 ■

# Conclusion:
# Looking Ahead to
# New Forms of Training and Managing

In the 1950s, when I entered the corporate world, we Americans generally regarded ourselves as the best in very nearly everything: in productivity, in quality, in managerial wisdom. In the 1970s, when that self-portrait began to show signs of considerable wear and tear, it was sad to see the confidence flow out of us. (And it didn't help that we lost a war at the same time.) Of course, there was plenty of blame to go around. Managers had always said that the unions were ruining the country. The unions charged managements with greed and shortsightedness. In training we often heard complaints that managers didn't understand the value of training and wouldn't bring the human resource people into the planning process. The managers, on the other hand, could be heard to complain that people sat on their backsides in the training department and made little effort to understand their concerns and needs.

Then came the Japanese, fortunately, so that we could blame almost everything on them. We had overlooked several years of warnings from Peter Drucker, who wrote consistently in the *Wall Street Journal* that the Japanese were indeed coming and they were a distinct threat. But now we can bash the Japanese, a sport somewhat tinged with racism. We can also perspire a bit over the colossus that the new reunited Germany will constitute. There will be no end of people to blame.

But the real culprit was our complacency. I've already admitted to distrusting generalizations, but here's one anyway. If I were to characterize our business activity of the 1950s, 1960s, and 1970s, I would say that most of us were effective in spite of ourselves. Mind you, I don't think we were terribly efficient. We didn't take strategy all that seriously (with a few notable exceptions); we had layers upon layers of management; we spent money cyclically. When the economy was great, we spent lavishly. Then we'd have a downturn, and it was "watch the pennies." Trainers got very used to the cycles. Every few years the training department would be wiped out, only to be reconstituted when prosperity was deemed to have returned.

We had planning departments to tell us where we might be in five years, but any relationship between their projections and where we actually were was often accidental. Still, we made money—that meant we were effective but not efficient. Then came a time, not many years ago, when some of us couldn't make money no matter what we did. We were obsolete: in our thinking, our planning, our producing, our attention to details.

### A Concern for Efficiency

My own corporate world was a microcosm of America. We had a remarkable flow of information, much of it informal and through the grapevine, but there wasn't much of a dialogue between divisions and departments. And I suspect that was fairly typical of the organizations of the day. Although I had a sales and marketing background, my suggestions and opinions regarding my company's marketing were not welcomed once I had become a member of the editorial (production) group. I watched in growing horror as sales and marketing decisions were made that I knew spelled big trouble for us. But the word was clear: Butt out. We're not interested in what you think.

That attitude pervaded the three editorial departments. There was little talking back and forth and a dearth of collaboration. There was much duplication of effort, since no one wanted to admit a dependence on others. Time after time I read newsletters and reports that the other departments put out that mine should have, since we had the specialists in those areas. But I suspected that the other departments preferred to risk a bad piece of work rather than call on us.

Such a deplorable condition was hardly unique to us. Marketing did its thing; production did its thing; finance did its thing; and so on. The lead time for new products is still sometimes two and three times what it is for foreign companies that have learned to bring all relevant departments together for simultaneous inputs and decisions. On our side of the ocean, it was not unusual for R&D to come up with a new product design; then engineering would look at it and make changes; then it was back to R&D, and out again, this time to production, where further changes were required. Then finance had a crack at it, perhaps marketing, and on and on. It was all in sequence, of course. It took forever, because no one had the wisdom or the courage to suggest that project teams representing the various functions work together. But, stumbling as we did, my company made money and managed to put out some pretty good products. That was true of the rest of the country. And that was just dandy, as long as we pretty much had the arena to ourselves. Then we found that others were playing better ball in our ballpark.

Meanwhile, in my company, we had a change of management. And now, the emphasis was on efficiency. Suddenly we were working with lots of new rules, regulations, and procedures. Not even the grapevine worked very well. Top management apparently came to the conclusion that replacing a highly paid editor with two lesser paid people would result in twice as much output. It didn't work that way, but it must have seemed like an efficient idea.

Well, the upshot of this painful story is that we lost whatever effectiveness we had had. We might have lost it anyway; the whole climate was changing. A lot of businesses lost it, without necessarily becoming efficient.

It seems to me that we in American business have lost much time and much ground. All that training and development of managers hasn't paid off, primarily because it wasn't terribly effective. Actually, much of it was very efficient. I've seen some elaborate curricula in my time, and there sure have been innumerable glitzy presentations. I'll bet no trainers in the whole world are as good as we are in presenting multimedia productions. But as I have said, ad nauseam, efficiency doesn't always lead to effectiveness. Good training delivery and methodology don't always lead to improved performance. Sophisticated theories don't always lend themselves to easy application.

We haven't been talking with one another as we should have. The trainers have been here, and management has been there, and we've done a poor job of bridging the gap between us.

### ASTD Task Force

To ensure that the American Society for Training and Development remained the point organization in promoting human resource development, in early 1988 President William N. Yeomans formed a task force of high-level corporate training executives and experienced consultants to tackle the continuing need to integrate HRD into business. Behind the formation of this knowledgeable group was the recognition that the United States faced enormous challenges in the global economy—and was not doing all that well. From the unpublished report of the task force came these words, referring to American business: "Management know-how, once strongly identified with America's vaunted leadership, has become the strength of the industrial bases of countries in Europe and Asia as well." And the paragraph concluded with a zinger: "The U.S. quite simply and frequently finds itself outpriced and outproduced." I'm not sure at the time that we seriously considered the impact of 1992 in Europe, but it is threatening.

The report advanced the following reason to explain our growing competitive disadvantage: "In many American businesses, investments in training and education have largely grown haphazardly and tend to be decentralized and poorly evaluated as to their cost effectiveness." There were, according to the task force, four inadequacies that needed to be addressed:

1. "First, there is a tendency by management to view training as a luxury expense." That attitude is probably a legacy of the glory days when our businesses made money, in the words of an executive client of mine in the 1960s, "no matter what we did." I suspect that, for much of American business, that conceit persisted into the 1980s. After all, if you make money whatever you do, training becomes one

of those nice things to do. But when the economy turns down, get rid of that cost center known as the training department.

2. "Second, the task force believes that training in most organizations is often determined by the values of the most important person, usually the CEO." But the important person can be anyone who controls the training budget and has responsibility for authorizing the training. Sometimes the training department operates on its own, developing programs and curricula that may have little relationship to the mission of the company. Trainers who work in such an environment tend to get very wrapped up in the inputs and the means rather than the outputs and the ends.

3. "A third inadequacy to be addressed involves trainers' perceptions of themselves as 'second-class' members of the organization." I've addressed that miserable perception earlier in the book. If you feel powerless, you are unlikely to try to spread your influence. You must be a maverick and a pioneer. And a discontent. Organizations don't encourage such pioneering, but it can be done if you know how to build your power base.

4. "Finally, in examining the issue of HRD and business, the task force recognizes that many people coming into the HRD field originated in the public sector or have, in their career history, focused on 'development theory' rather than on business practice." In short, they run schools rather than help to run the business.

*For the Manager.* You can easily recognize why my sitting on this task force was immensely gratifying for me. It was comforting for me to see that many of my professional colleagues share some of my misgivings and complaints.

There were a number of recommendations developed for the business CEO to help increase the impact and value of the training done in the company. But for the most part, you can see that the recommendations apply widely in management, not just at the top. Following are a selection from and a condensation of these recommendations to line management:

- The responsibility and accountability for development belong with line management, and all such T&D should be connected with operating and strategic planning.

- Training is part of the total performance system: application on the job, appraisal, rewards.
- Stay close to the providers of T&D to ensure that what is delivered is in line with strategic objectives.
- In partnership with your HRD professional, establish priorities for training and schedules for achieving them. Measure usefulness in outputs, not inputs.
- Select HRD professionals who demonstrate a knowledge of the business and the culture, who can identify problems and work toward solutions, who can stand up to managers who want training that does not contribute to the achievement of strategic objectives, and who view training as a systemwide approach to increasing competitiveness.
- Insist on measurable results from the training.
- Use nontraining personnel.

*For the Trainer.* Now to balance the books, here are some of the recommendations for the HRD professional:

- Learn how to communicate effectively with your organizational clients by using their language and respecting their priorities.
- Establish the link between training and business requirements. Be able to show that training is cost-effective.
- Acquire power and influence through alliances with key individuals, association with power centers, building credibility through professional competence, getting results through consistent delivery of quality performance, and helping others to achieve power and influence (the trainers' reward power).
- Involve functional managers and other clients in the responsibility for training.
- Develop and demonstrate an understanding of the total organization, its strategy, the environment in which it operates.
- Keep training client-centered, not client- or trainer-dominated.
- Find new problems you can solve.
- Use your unique position of influence and perspective to bring parties together to address pervasive problems and strategic needs, since these often transcend functions and lines of authority.

- Know the field and technology of training, for competence is the primary source of your power and influence.

Not bad. The work of this task force has a lot of credibility, made up as it was of senior professionals, many of whom had extensive corporate experience. And it pleases me that they share many of my conclusions, biases, and advice.

### Looking to the Future

*The Business World of the Fifties.* To paraphrase Abraham Lincoln, the traditions of the past are inadequate for the present—and especially for the future. It's a popular tradition, when approaching a new decade, to talk about the many changes that will take place in it, the new challenges and opportunities. It's a tradition well founded in 1990, as I write. We have a far different environment, work force, corporate profile, from when I entered the business world in the early 1950s, when it was a much simpler world, as I've often described. The usual corporation was the pyramid, a sharp point at the top, a broadness at the bottom. Communications were generally top down. Whatever went up was carefully controlled by the chain of command, just as in the military; there was little horizontal talking. When I went into the field as a group insurance specialist for my company, mine was one of perhaps twenty-five offices in the United States. We didn't have the phone numbers of the other offices. No one saw any justification for our talking with other specialists. When representatives of other divisions or departments in the home office visited my city, they saw no reason to pick up the phone and say "hello."

The reward systems were very simple and uncomplicated. It was assumed that most people had one priority: to earn money to buy a house, a car, a vacation, country club membership, and so on. We were pyramid climbers and status seekers, as Vance Packard (1964) would write in his book of the same name.

Most older corporations were paternalistic, and you as employee were loyal. It wasn't unusual for you to have the pension plan explained to you even though you were twenty-five instead of sixty-five. People weren't very mobile. You married the corporation, and the corporation took care of you. Your career was usually synonymous with your tenure in the corporation you joined right out of school or the service.

You certainly didn't hear such phrases as cultural diversity, which is very much in vogue now. Almost everyone above the blue-collar and clerical levels was white and male. It was a uniform world; it was also a conforming world. We didn't really use the word *culture* to describe our companies, but we knew that every corporation had its way of doing things, and you had better do them the prescribed way. Mavericks were not well tolerated. I well remember my boss sitting in my office and saying, in puzzlement and frustration, "You're not like all the others," meaning the other group insurance specialists. I didn't last much longer.

For many, it was a comfortable, well-defined, and well-structured world. You knew the rules and followed them. Everyone in the corporate hierarchy knew the status of everyone else. There was little ambiguity. Many of these people found the restlessness and hostility of the young people in the 1960s very threatening and tragic. Others of us who had grown to find the world of the 1950s to be stifling were less disturbed. We even appreciated the irony. My boss laughed one day: "These kids want nothing to do with the establishment. All we could think about was getting into it." True.

*Cultural Changes.* We no longer exist and have to work in such a buttoned-down world. Someone remarked to me the other day, rather pontifically, "Paternalism is dead." That's just fine. Paternalism was condescending, offensive to our dignity, and in the final days, unjust and uncaring. Now we live and work in a more chancy world. It certainly is much more complicated. Those orderly levels of management are gone in most companies, and so are many of the rules. Even the white shirts have given way to colors. We now deal with people of many backgrounds with different values: Asians, African-Americans, Hispanics, women who don't believe they have to imitate men, young people with M.B.A.s and Ph.Ds. Loyalty is gone. Mobility is in, although you may concern yourself with vesting.

We now recognize that people work to achieve many kinds of goals, not just the house, the car, the vacation. We have employees who insist on knowing what is going on in the corporation and not always believing what management chooses to tell them. *Self-actualization* was an esoteric term when Maslow introduced it back in the 1950s. But now a lot of people seem to feel it is their right to become what they are capable of becoming, and if they can't achieve it in one place, they look for it in another. Most employees have come to realize that their primary loyalty is to themselves.

I remember the days when we had just the information we needed and little more. Now there is so much information that we nearly drown in it, and much of it contradicts the rest. Where is our well-ordered world? It was an illusion, as much as the one that says good managers are decisive and the best decisions are rational. In reality, indecisiveness can be a virtue, and most good decisions are nonrational.

In 1968, Warren Bennis, in his book *The Temporary Society* (Bennis and Slater, 1968), advocated more open, adaptable organizations with the liberal use of temporary groups such as task forces and project teams. But he worried that American managers would have a low tolerance for ambiguity. Well, we are moving toward more flexible organizational structure. We had better get used to leaderless teams and self-directed work groups. If we don't have a high tolerance for ambiguity we'll all go mad. This is not a stable, ordered, highly structured world any longer.

*New Challenges for Managers.* We're moving, at long last, closer to the profile of the effective organization envisioned by the late Rensis Likert, who more than anyone in the 1950s and 1960s championed participative management. He defined it as "System 4: Participative Group" (1961). Here's how I describe the System 4 organization in my book *How People Work Best* (1988a, p. 52): "Management trusts employees, regards them as working willingly toward the achievement of organizational objectives. People are motivated by rewards. At all levels they are involved in discussing and deciding those issues that are important to them. Communication is quite accurate and goes up, down, and across. Goals are not ordered from on high but are set with the participation of the people who will have to work to achieve them. Informal organizations are benign: they support the formal organization."

Likert proposed a "linking pin" structure of organization. Each work group—defined as a manager and all subordinates who report to him or her—is part of a larger group, which in turn is part of an even larger group. In this way, everyone in the organization is connected with everyone else. In Likert's words, it's an "Interaction-Influence System: highly effective work groups linked together by other highly effective work groups" (1961).

Here are the patterns that such an organization would show, according to the eminent social scientist:

- Each member of the organization would be loyal not only to his or her own work group but to the organization as a whole. [Is it possible that we shall see a return of loyalty to the organization? Likert thought so.]
- Through the overlapping groups, each member would be able to exert influence on all parts of the organization.
- Every member would believe that the values and goals of both his or her own group and the organization as a whole adequately reflected the member's own values and goals. Thus, the accomplishment of the group's and organization's goals would be the best way to meet his or her own needs and personal goals.
- Important information would flow to the points in the organization where the information is relevant for decisions and actions.
- All relevant information would flow to the points at which decisions are made [Likert, 1961, p. 183].

"The nearer the system of a particular company approaches this ideal," Likert (1961) wrote, "the better will be the communication, decision-making and motivation processes of the organization."

It's very close to what Douglas McGregor (1960) said in his Theory Y—that most people will direct themselves to achieving objectives to which they are committed. The commitment has much to do with the rewards that are associated with the achievement of those objectives.

## The New Democracy

Unquestionably, we are moving to a flatter, more open, more flexible and decentralized organization—slowly but surely. One of my favorite quotations dates from 1968 when Warren Bennis (1968, p. 4) wrote, "Democracy becomes a functional necessity whenever a social system is competing for survival under conditions of chronic change." Does that feel right? Certainly our corporations are competing for survival, and the Communists in middle and eastern Europe are discovering this reality.

Management is changing. More power to the people, more decision-making authority, less so-called managerial authority, more management by negotiation and persuasion, less unilateral action, and more group decisions. It's a long way from the management world I first knew in 1954.

Bennis was leading up to suggesting that the work groups, on which Likert places so much importance, will be increasingly, but not totally, temporary. There will be more temporary problem-solving groups, more project teams, more self-managed work groups.

In my book *Your Role in Task Force Management* (1972, p. 200), I wrote the following astonishingly confident words:

> But we cannot ignore that the revolution is already upon us. Our organizations have to be able to cope with the values of the new work force. . . . If our technology is not to outstrip our ability to utilize it for our own sake, we must have effective ways to train people in the problem-solving and decision-making skills that are requisite to handle it. We cannot close our eyes to the information explosion and our need to know.
>
> We can expect more theory, more experiential learning. Undoubtedly in time we shall enjoy better tools. In the meantime, we should take advantage of

what we already know, the tools that are available to us now.

The task force . . . is a tool that has proved successful. We know what can be accomplished with it, even though relatively few organizations have made extensive use of it [this was 1972, remember]. We already know how to train people to be effective on task forces. We can recognize that the task force as a concept and as a technique goes *with* the grain of the forces of change in business [ah, yes]. We know that widespread use of the task force can help us control, advance and benefit from the revolution that promises to transform our society.

The future is already here. It is up to us to make it work.

A bit premature. I was, however, correct, I think, in arguing the necessity of a more open, less structured, responsive, and decentralized organization for the sake of effectiveness and adaptability. The work group has become tremendously important. The participation of its members in the decision making of the work group has become inevitable.

Do your training programs offer the skills that will be necessary in the new reality? It takes both management and HRD professionals to answer this question in the way it must be answered.

# ■ References ■

Argyris, C. *Executive Leadership*. New York: Harper & Row, 1953.

"ASTD Task Force on Integrating HRD into Business." Unpublished manuscript. Alexandria, Va.: American Society for Training and Development, 1988.

Bennis, W., and Slater, P. *The Temporary Society*. New York: Harper & Row, 1968.

Blake, R., and Mouton, J. *The Managerial Grid*. Houston, Tex.: Gulf, 1964.

Herzberg, F. *Work and the Nature of Man*. Cleveland, Ohio: World, 1966.

Likert, R. *New Patterns of Management*. New York: McGraw-Hill, 1961.

*Linking New Employee Attitudes and Values to Improved Productivity, Cost, and Quality*. Philadelphia: Hay Group, 1989.

McGregor, D. *The Human Side of Enterprise*. New York: McGraw-Hill, 1960.

M.I.T. Commission on Industrial Productivity. *Made in America*. Cambridge, Mass.: MIT Press, 1990.

Maslow, A. *Motivation and Personality*. New York: Harper & Row, 1954.

Odiorne, G. *Management by Objectives*. New York: Pitman, 1965.

Packard, V. *The Pyramid Climbers*. New York: Crest, 1964.

Quick, T. *Your Role in Task Force Management: The Dynamics of Corporate Change.* New York: Doubleday, 1972.

Quick, T. *The Persuasive Manager: How to Sell Yourself and Your Ideas.* Radnor, Pa.: Chilton, 1982.

Quick, T. *The Manager's Motivation Desk Book.* New York: Wiley, 1985.

Quick, T. *Inspiring People at Work: How to Make Participative Management Work for You.* New York: Executive Enterprises, 1986.

Quick, T. *How People Work Best.* New York: Executive Enterprises, 1988a.

Quick, T. *Power, Influence, and Your Effectiveness in Human Resources.* Reading, Mass.: Addison-Wesley, 1988b.

Quick, T. *Managing for Peak Performance.* New York: Executive Enterprises, 1989a.

Quick, T. *Unconventional Wisdom: Irreverent Solutions for Tough Problems at Work.* San Francisco: Jossey-Bass, 1989b.

Quick, T. *Mastering the Power of Persuasion: How to Get the Results You Want on the Job.* New York: Executive Enterprises, 1990.

Shaw, M. *Assertive-Responsive Management.* Reading, Mass.: Addison-Wesley, 1979.

Vroom, V. *Work and Motivation.* New York: Wiley, 1964.

*Wall Street Journal.* Interview with W. Edwards Deming. June 4, 1990, special supplement, p. 1.

Whyte, W., Jr. *The Organization Man.* New York: Simon & Schuster, 1956.

# ■ Index ■

185